Prayers of the People

Pastoral Prayers for Worship and Personal Devotion

by

Richard Einerson

Bloomington, IN Milton Keynes, UK

authorHOUSE

AuthorHouse™
1663 Liberty Drive, Suite 200
Bloomington, IN 47403
www.authorhouse.com
Phone: 1-800-839-8640

AuthorHouse™ UK Ltd.
500 Avebury Boulevard
Central Milton Keynes, MK9 2BE
www.authorhouse.co.uk
Phone: 08001974150

First published by AuthorHouse 5/3/2006

ISBN: 1-4259-2598-7 (sc)

Printed in the United States of America
Bloomington, Indiana

This book is printed on acid-free paper.

The source material for the readings is from The Revised Common Lectionary;
a Vanderbilt Divinity Library Online Resource. Used with permission.

Scripture quotations are from the New Revised Standard Version of the Bible,
©1989 by the Division of Christian Education of the National Council of
Churches of Christ in the USA. Used with Permission. All rights reserved.

Most of these prayers are based on the common lectionary as maintained by The Library at Vanderbilt University Divinity School.

Dedications

For Carolyn, my spouse of over fifty years
and my friend, who has always been
encouraging in my writing this book;

for our oldest daughter Stephanie, husband
Bob Narveson, and granddaughter *Krista
Lynn*
in Minnesota;

for our twin daughter Sonia and husband
Jerry Holland, musicians in San Francisco;
(www.sonyholland.com.)

for our second twin daughter Andrea,
husband John Lende, and grandsons:
John Andrew
James Alexander,
Jacob Austin,
in Colorado;

all of whom bring great joy!

Foreward

The idea for this book was conceived after many people encouraged me to write my prayers. The prayers in this book are mostly based on the universal common lectionary. For the lay person the lectionary is a group of usually four texts: a Psalm, an Old Testament lesson, a New Testament lesson, and a Gospel lesson. One of the four is usually designated as the suggested preaching text for the Sunday scheduled. I have used the lectionary maintained by the Library of the Vanderbilt University Divinity School which was suggested to me as an excellent source. A second reason for using the lectionary from Vanderbilt was that I had a Danforth Foundation grant in 1959-60 and spent a year there with powerful memories. That year happened to be the year the South began to experience accelerated social change with the "sit ins."

From what I have read the Presbyterians have often intentionally put a tap on the shoulder of its young people who tend to show talent which would enhance their ministry. In a way this book was kind of a tap on the shoulder from the community. In semi-retirement I spent a number of years as a Pastoral Associate at the Palm Desert Community Presbyterian Church where many people commented favorably upon and requested my prayers. The same held true when I served as an Interim Associate Pastor at Plymouth Congregational Church in Ft. Collins, Colorado. The encouragement from both communities was decisive in my decision to proceed with this work.

I can't in a foreward address the philosophical issues or questions people may have about prayer. When I was a chaplain at Meritcare Medical Center in Fargo, North Dakota I was frequently asked by patients to pray for a "miracle." A time of crisis is hardly a time to discuss issues about prayer. I told them I was not in the guarantee side of prayer but I had no hesitation to ask. Some got what they asked for. For others praying was a process which led to further dialogue and negotiation with God. In either case we put ourselves and our concerns up front with God.

My own notion about prayer is that when we pray we put ourselves and our passions strongly on the side of our requests. And frequently we hear passions we ought to hold, but do not quite yet, which come from the Scriptures. I will give two examples. One Sunday late in 2003 a woman by the name of Margaret Stockover at Plymouth Congregational Church asked me for a copy of the morning pastoral prayer which I immediately copied and gave to her. Margaret went that winter to Afghanistan to assist women without husbands who were disenfranchised from economic opportunity and had no way to provide for themselves. She taught them to sew and sell their goods and to provide for themselves. She later told me that the prayer which she requested that Sunday was what helped her decide that she must go to Afghanistan. I admired her courage. I am not sure I would be so courageous. She has since gone back twice to Afghanistan A second like experience happened when a young black student got up during the sharing of joys and concerns and announced that he was going into a very difficult graduate program. He said he developed courage for this decision when he heard the Associate Pastor praying to God the previous Sunday to give us difficult challenges. Experiences like this reinforce for me the importance of worship and prayer in the life of the church today.

Many of the prayers in this book are focused around the suggested text of the day. There are some which only nod to the text. And there is a small number which are written without regard to the text because of a particular theme of the day which is developed. There are several texts from Samuel which were suggested texts for preaching and I have chosen instead to do a prayer on one of the New Testament lessons. Many of the prayers for year C (2007) were written while I was at Plymouth Congregational Church in Fort Collins, CO. So the year C prayers are built around the texts of 2004.

I am usually accustomed to end a prayer with reference to Jesus. I have chosen in most instances not to use my usual prayer ending and instead will leave it up the reader or pastor to choose the ending most appropriate for her/him.

During the several years in which these prayers were written in final form the world experienced many serious natural disasters. I have chosen in a few instances to leave those in the prayers because of the overwhelming power of the human suffering involving so many people.

The task of writing these prayers for publication has provided a very significant personal and unanticipated side benefit. Living with and working with three years of texts in a period of thirteen months has been itself good for my own soul. It once again has reinforced for me the value in engagement with the Scriptures. It is my hope that the readers and users will in some measure find the personal enrichment which has come to me. If the book is used for personal devotion I would recommend reading all of the texts suggested. If time permits only one to be read then the text which is highlighted (bold) and underlined should be read.

Finally, I wish to express some words of appreciation. First, my thanks to The Rev. Hal Chorpenning, Senior Pastor, Plymouth Congregational Church, for encouraging me in this venture, for directing me to publishers I could afford, and for designing the book cover. Second, my thanks are extended to Plymouth Congregational Church for their very generous gift when I was finished with my interim time there, and which was intended for and covered my publishing costs. My time with them greatly enriched my life and faith. Third, to all those who through the years graciously received me as their pastor or chaplain and who inspired me with their faithfulness; and to my colleagues over the years who have nurtured me in personal and professional growth, I owe profound gratitude.

Richard J. Einerson

<u>YEAR A</u>

<u>First Sunday of Advent</u>   **<u>Isaiah 2:1-5</u>**   Psalm 122

November 28, 2004   Romans 13:11-14   Matthew 24:36-44

Eternal God, as we begin another advent season, help us to be faithful to the ancient vision. May we find in our hearts that ancient vision of the mountain of the Lord whereby we may be taught your ways and walk in your paths.

- Make us more teachable.
- Make us more inwardly changeable.
- Make us hunger for the Word which is eternal.
- Make us renewed people who are able to give up the ways of war, force, and violence as ways to solve conflicts.
- Make us as nations willing to give up the sword for plowshares, spears for pruning hooks, armored vehicles for tractors and vehicles of transportation, guns for computers, ammunition for food.

Make this advent season a season of quiet retooling of our own souls. Shake up our values. Cause us to commit our energies to making this world a place where there is greater justice for all peoples and where all your people have a place to live in safety and have adequate food and nutrition. Cause us to create a world where there is less cause for resentment, where there is less cause for terrorists to seek their own kind of redress for the world's wrongs, and where there is a diminished chasm between the world of those who have and those who have not.

As we prepare the way of the Lord we pray that you will keep in your gentle care all those in our world who suffer. Be with the lonely, those who go to bed hungry, the refugees and the displaced. May they all be touched by your compassionate love. Amen

Eternal God, we come to you during this season of hope. May the power of Jesus be born in us again.

- Rekindle that power in those who have grown weary.
- Restore hope to those whose present or past lives have become a burden.
- Renew within us the vision and excitement of lives which are motivated, which have a sense of mission, and which are directed toward a lofty purpose.

If any is imprisoned in a past which is crippling or which tenaciously diminishes new possibilities for today, provide a way of reframing that past so that it no longer imprisons, so that it can be transcended, so that it can be seen as an asset rich with the ability to understand the human experience and relate to the sufferings of others.

You come, gentle Jesus, to a world of broken people. Come again to us and transform us as you did those who experienced your touch and your grace. May some new truth excite us, may the possibility of some new loving behaviour look achievable, and may some new vision claim us.

We pray for those who need your special touch: those who are ill; those for whom the season causes sadness or depression; those who are lonely; those who are on our prayer list; those whose lives are forever compromised by frailty of the body and who will never be fully active again. We pray also for our world: confused, in constant strife, filled with passions and rage and uncertainty. Hold this world in your compassionate embrace. Enable us as a global people to care for one another and to see those who are different from us less as threats and enemies and more as your loving children. May a new world be born. Amen

Third Sunday of Advent   **Isaiah 35:1-10**   Psalm 146:5-10 or *Luke 1:47-55*
December 12, 2004   James 5:7-10   John 1:6-8, 19-28

Our gracious, eternal God, energize our weary spirits this day. Fill us with the ancient vision of Isaiah so that the wilderness of our lives and the desert places of our spirits and the badlands of our interior space might celebrate and blossom. May we behold your awesome love for all peoples.

We confess that we often are a weak-kneed and fearful people. We are fearful and anxious of heart.

- We are often anxious about our tomorrows.
- We are anxious about our health.
- We are anxious and fearful of our own interior shadow and darkness, fearful to embrace it and simply to say: "you too are a part of my being."
- We are anxious and fearful about our body politic where statesmanship often yields to unbridled power and self-interest.
- We are anxious about our world where there seems always to be so much hostility.

We find comfort that Isaiah's world, simple and much less sophisticated than ours, also had fearful people. Imprint his message in our hearts and souls this day. Help us to be strong and not to fear. May we find courage enough for each difficult experience. May we find the resolve to choose to receive grace enough just for today and to trust you for tomorrow.

In this advent preparation time help us to prepare for new comings of your holy one. May we be open to and grasped by a new truth so that we may fulfill our complete destiny as a part of your redeemed people. May we reach out to those in need and resolve to contribute to making this a better world where all obtain greater joy and gladness. May all peoples be captured by a new vision of love and peace. Amen.

3

God, we come to you toward the end of this season of hope. We thank you for our annual journey to Bethlehem. Help us to learn anew Bethlehem's lessons. Help us to know this long ago and eagerly hoped for child called Emmanuel. You came, Lord Jesus, to a world of broken people. Come again to us. Enable us to see you in the broken whom we meet and to minister to them in your name. Lead us again to receive you who were known as Emmanuel, God with us. May we know that you are indeed with us.

- May we know you are with us in our moments of boredom and disinterest.
- May we know you are with us in our homes and families.
- May we know you are with us in our sufferings.
- May we know you are with us in our triumphs but also our defeats.
- May we know that you are in the events of life and the God of history.

O COME, O COME, EMMANUEL!

- Come and make yourself known to the little people of the world.
- Come and make yourself known to the forgotten and the powerless.
- Come and make yourself known to the powerful who are confident in their own powers and who often do not see their need of you.
- Come and make yourself known to the leaders of this world and give them a vision of a world at peace.
- Come and make yourself known in all of the darkest places of human life.

O COME, O COME, EMMANUEL! Amen

4

Eternal God, we bow in awe this holy night. On our journey through advent, like so many previous advent seasons, we still come to this Christmas eve and bow in wonder, awe, and adoration. We bow before your mystery. The wonder and mystery of your workings in Jesus continue to astound and surprise us. We are surprised by his coming into our world in such an unexpected place. We are surprised by his coming to an unexpecting mother. We are surprised by his coming in such an unheralded way and so unnoticed by most of the nations of the earth.

Like the ancients we thank you that Jesus is an ever-present voice crying out to us:

- reminding us that the dry places of life hold within them a sense of promise;
- reminding us that despair need only be momentary and not a permanent place of dwelling for our souls;
- reminding us that the worst of times have always the potential to draw from within us the best of our resources and abilities;
- reminding us that the darkness can never overcome the light and that hope can never be extinguished from the human breast.

BE PRESENT WITH US IN OUR JOURNEY, GENTLE JESUS.

Be also with those whose hope is diminished this Christmas time. Be with the homeless, the weary, the over-worked, the unemployed, the hungry, the refugees, all suffering children everywhere, the grieving. Be with those who live in lands where there is war and strife and who suffer innocently. Be with our soldiers far from home. Bring us peace and cradle this world of yours in your special love. Amen

Eternal God, we thank you that in the fullness of time you came among us in Jesus and visited us with your grace. We thank you that you forever hold us in your loving embrace. Yet we are reminded by the flight of Mary and Joseph to Egypt that there is a continuing battle between principalities and powers and that when the powerful are threatened horrific evil can result and innocent people suffer. We pray for those who suffer innocently.

As we look at a new year we are also aware of the fragility of life. Make us also aware of the prayer of the Psalmist who said: "Teach us to number our days that we may gain a heart of wisdom." Our reflections on the mystery of time always create anxiety within us, for we know that our days are numbered and there will be a time when we are no more. In such anxious moments help us to place our trust in you, the eternal rock of ages.

Be with those for whom time has become a burden and for whom time seems to stand still.

- Be with those whose strength is diminishing.
- Be with those who can no longer engage the world beyond their own walls and are confined to their homes or a living center.
- Be with those who suffer from illnesses which slowly destroy the mind and quietly but persistently steal a person from his or her family.
- Be with those who grieve and feel as if they have been cheated of more good time with their loved one and who feel that their best life is past.

Be present with them all and grant them your gracious comfort.

Be also in all of the troubled spots of earth and lead all nations to work for peace. Help us all to temper our hatreds and learn your ways of love. Amen

Eternal God, you in whom all beginnings are a mystery but in whom also was the "Word," your creative passion to create and to communicate, we thank you for your Word made flesh. We thank you that in that Word there was life bringing light to all people. May your Word continue to penetrate our beings and our behaviours. We are grateful today.

- We are grateful for the richness of the Biblical witness and its reminders of the potential we hold within us.
- We are grateful for the reminders of the heavenly vision which leads us onward and causes us to grow and to reach for gains not yet realized.
- We are grateful for the reminders that our lives are intended for rich community, fellowship, and responsible service.

We ask for your continued care for a greater mastery of life. Help us to lean upon you and find strength for our journey.

- When we are timid give us courage.
- When we are anxious give us peace.
- When we falter gently nudge us to continue
- When we are offended enable us to forgive.
- When we are discouraged uplift our spirits.

As we lean into this new year lead us to a deeper understanding of your Word made flesh. Give us his compassion for the disadvantaged, the disenfranchised, the forgotten, the embittered. May we look for the Christ in these neighbours whom we usually forget. May we find new ways to love our sisters and brothers. Amen

Our gracious God, we thank you this day for the opportunity to worship and open our souls to you. As Jesus was baptized we too need the newness of life and the rebirth which it symbolizes. For we have many needs. And we have many behaviours which look considerably less than baptized. We have many things to confess.

- We nurture slights and become preoccupied with how ill-willed some people are.
- We hold onto old wrongs which feel like weights on our spirits.
- We worry about tomorrow as if you will not go before us.
- We draw erroneous conclusions from others' behaviour or words which are based only on our faulty perceptions.
- We insist on our own way.

O God, be with us on our journey because our souls need regular re-working. Help us to know that it truly is we who stand in the need of prayer.

Help us to find healing for our own souls in order that we may put aside the baggage of the past which weighs so heavily upon us. Help us to try new and more generous behaviours which are filled with love and good will. Help us to withhold our judgments until we truly understand.

Instead of asking for life to be all smooth sailing give us the courage to ask for challenges. Instead of cowering before difficulty give us the strength to stretch for greater mastery of greater challenges.

Again we ask your gracious mercy upon those whose lives are disrupted by illness, uncertainty, and death. And swing low over all those whose souls are so encapsulated in hatred that they can only wish to kill and maim and hurt their fellow human beings. Amen

Second Sunday after the Epiphany   Isaiah 49:1-7 Psalm 40:1-11
January 16, 2005   I Corinthians 1:1-9 **John 1:29-42**

Eternal God, whose majesty is beyond our comprehension; whose love is so great, so broad, so deep and so high, that we cannot imagine it; cast your loving spell over the earth these days.

Melt the hatreds of humankind which we think we cannot live without and which we so carefully nurture. Dispel the notions within any of your children that cause them to feel that they have been permanently wronged. And dispel the illusion that by hurting another anything can be made right. Jesus taught us a better way, a way of hungering and thirsting after righteousness, which your children have struggled with for centuries. Right the wrongs in our thinking and in our behaviours. Instead of pointing fingers of blame at others may all the earth be softened by your love so that we may say and claim with the old spiritual, that is we "O Lord, standing in the need of prayer."

Hover over those places of special need where there is human suffering, conflict, and war. Penetrate those dark places with your light that the world may achieve a new order and harmony.

Help us to hear again the simple invitation Jesus gave to his disciples when they wondered what he was all about. May we hear again the words of the excited disciple: "Come and see."

- Help us to come and see this one whom the prophet John called "the lamb of God who takes away the sin of the world."
- Help us to come and see and explore the calling of our spirits to make sense out of life and to make life commitments.
- Help us to come and see the tasks to which Jesus calls us in our time.
- Help us to come and see and be transformed as was Peter.

O God, help us to "come and see" and trust. Amen

9

Third Sunday after the Epiphany Isaiah 9:1-4   Psalm 24:1, 4-9
January 23, 2005   I Corinthians 1:10-18   **Matthew 4:12-23**

Eternal God, strong to save, we come to you with divided hearts. We would wish to escape the constant din of war and hatred and grief which infects the earth but we cannot for there is nowhere to hide. We would wish to escape the darker sides of our own nature which entice us to wish and long for more than justice and want revenge for evil people. This day may we affirm with Paul our powerlessness on the one hand. But let us not linger there.

- Help us to affirm with him: *"Thanks be to God through our Lord Jesus Christ!"*
- Help us in this process not to become like our enemies.
- Help us in this time to turn more deeply to you, to affirm again that we will be your followers, to respond as did your disciples to your bidding: *"Follow me."*
- Calm the angry waves of our souls with your words: *"Peace, be still."*
- Teach us anew that this, and every day, is a day which you have made, and we **will** choose to rejoice and be glad in it.
- Deepen our realization that you are the rock of ages, and that we cling to you for strength and transformation.

We ask your gentle care in those war torn areas of our world. We pray for the uprooted, the refugees, the hungry, the children and all those innocents who find themselves in the wrong place at this very wrong time. Be with our armed forces as they daily are in danger. Be with our world leaders and cause them to be statesmen. Bend low your presence to all of the suffering and provide them with courage and a renewed hope for a better life. May we see a new world born. **Amen**

Fourth Sunday after the Epiphany Micah 6:1-8   Psalm 15
January 30, 2005   I Cor. 1:18-31   **Matthew 5:1-12**

Our gracious, eternal God, we cannot hear the words of Jesus without a profound sense of humility.

- We confess that our pride gets in the way of being poor in spirit.
- We confess that our desire for happiness is frustrated when we must grieve and we would rather have instant comfort.
- We confess that we do not trust that enough will come to us if we are meek so we expend too much aggressive energy into making sure that enough gets to our table.
- We confess that our hungers and thirsts are so great they keep us always striving for more.
- We confess that when it comes to mercy we are not always filled with grace. We want to get even when wronged.
- We confess that we are far from pure of heart and we play inwardly deceptive games to deny the depth and breadth of our own shadow and sinful side because of the terror of being found out for, or admitting, what we are.
- We confess that we are often not willing to make peace and we have no interest in being persecuted.

Help us this day to hear the gospel plainly. Help us to find some small ways in which we can make some gains and progress in our Christian endeavor. Accepted by your gracious love, help us to know that we are truly yours in spite of our shortcomings. And with that knowledge may we move forward boldly as your people.

We pray not only for ourselves but for all those whose situations are not as favorable as ours. Be with those who suffer, those whose lives are diminished by disease, those whose minds are anxious because of financial insecurity and inadequate means to provide for their needs, and those who are in harms way. Amen

Most gracious, eternal God, we come to you on this winter day aware that so much of our lives are flat, as if we live on a dreary plain. The daylight is diminished with shorter days of sunshine and we are aware of a restlessness within.

We pray that you might make us aware of your powerful and challenging presence. Lead us to your spiritual mountain as you led both Moses and Jesus.

- Lead us to your mountain and teach us to wait.
- Lead us to your mountain, and on our journey when the destination is not clear teach us also to walk in faith and trust.
- Lead us to your mountain even if it means going through haze, clouds and darkness to experience your power.
- Lead us to your mountain to find new truth and the truth of your law which we would have you burn into our souls.
- Lead us to your mountain where we might have a vision of peace among all of your warlike children.
- Lead us to your mountain where we might have a vision of a world remade:
  1. where all your children know justice;
  2. where all your children have the opportunity to have adequate food and nourishment;
  3. where all your children have the gift of literacy and reading great books;
  4. where all your children have the joy of meaningful work.

We pray for all those who have special needs: those at war away from family and friends; those who are ill; those facing life-threatening or chronic illness; those unemployed; those living in the shadows of depression. Grant them all your grace and strength and the courage to move forward to each new day. Amen

First Sunday in Lent   **Genesis 2:15-17; 3:1-7** Psalm 32
February 13, 2005   Romans 5:12-19   Matthew 4:1-11

O holy One, we bow this day aware of the great propensity for evil which exists among all humankind. We wish for an explanation of it but can only stand as did Job after he had asked all of his questions, and expended all of his fury, and realize we do not understand life's mysteries. Yet like the ancients who saw evil and who explained it in the simple story in the garden, who saw evil resulting from the sin of Adam and Eve, we know that we all have our gardens of evil. We all have known wrong-doing, guilt, and shame. We all are guilty. And we all share responsibility for the evil which is always so rampant among us. We cope so poorly with it.

- We would like to distance ourselves from it because it makes us so uncomfortable.
- We would like to use the mechanism of blame and project the evil bubbling within us onto others where it is more comfortable.
- We would like to remove the speck from our neighbour's eye and leave for another time the beam which is in our own eye.
- We would like to think that the troubles of the world reside in the waywardness of other nations of the world and not our own.
- We would like to absolve ourselves of responsibility because that would mean confronting the need for repentance.

Deliver us, gracious God, from the powers of darkness. Help us to find the honesty and courage which would enable us to look at our interior selves and own the truth. May we not fear the shadow within but embrace its reality. And in so doing may we discover the vastness of your redeeming love which is able to remove our transgressions, "as far as the east is from the west." May we become more gracious to our neighbours and more loving. We pray in your name. Amen

Second Sunday in Lent   **Genesis 12:1-4a**   **Psalm 121**
February 20, 2005   Romans 4:1-5,13-17   John 3:1-17 or *Matt. 17:1-9*

Our gracious, eternal God, we bow with thankful hearts. When we reflect upon life we can find a litany of things for which we are grateful.

- We are grateful for the splendour of stunningly beautiful sunsets.
- We are grateful for the quiet of winter.
- We are grateful for the beautiful clouds, for rainfall, for snow, for Lent and for the hope of seeing flowers and crops and the green world which we are privileged to behold in spring and summer.
- We are grateful for the mountains to which when we look we cannot but help knowing from whence our help comes.

When we reflect upon our faith we again find reason for gratitude. We thank you for the upward vision to which you call us in Jesus Christ. We thank you for the self-giving love to which his life was committed and the ideal of loving others to which we have been called. Be also our redeemer when we fall short of that ideal.

- When we feel enmity or hatred toward others remind us of our need to love and temper our spirits.
- When we act selfishly remind us of our need to consider others.
- When we are seeking to impose our will upon others remind us to listen to and hear the needs of those around us.
- And when we are inclined to keep the circle of those whom we love small remind us that love demands a wider justice for all of your children.

Cause love to abound among us and cause it to be contagious for our world. Cause us to serve you with joy and eager enthusiasm. Amen

14

Third Sunday in Lent   **Exodus 17:1-7**   Psalm 95
February 27, 2005   Romans 5:1-11   John 4:5-42

O holy One, always calling your people on a journey, we bow this day so aware of our similarity to the peoples of the past. The Israelites journeyed through the wilderness. Life for us often seems like a wilderness. They grumbled and complained. We too grumble and complain. We too live in those places called Massah and Meribah and wonder as did they: "Is the Lord among us or not?" We often feel unsure of our answer. We sometimes wonder where on earth we are going; why on earth we do what we do. We are unclear if you are leading us or perhaps we are just going along anyway. The temptation to return to the familiarity and comfort of an Egypt past is strong.

O holy One, we need your guidance and help.

- When the way seems dark and unclear give us enough light to find courage to take another step.
- When we are frightened and fearful give us enough courage not to falter.
- When we seem to be wandering give us enough assurance and trust to believe that in some way you are still leading us.
- When life is overwhelming give us enough strength to continue our journey.
- When our will and determination is low give us enough perseverance to continue.

O God, we wish to be faithful to the heavenly vision. We wish to reach out and embrace those with human needs and alleviate human suffering. Give us enough victories to keep us from despair and cynicism. Give us enough satisfaction and fulfillment to make it worth the effort. And even when it seems as if we are stepping forward into the darkness give us enough faith to know that you will always meet us there. Amen

Fourth Sunday in Lent   **I Samuel 16:1-13**   Psalm 23
March 6, 2005   Ephesians 5:8-14   John 9:1-41

Eternal God, we come before you with a mixture of feelings and a need of confession.

- We hear of the sufferings of Jesus yet resist hardship for ourselves.
- We set high expectations for others but resist them for ourselves.
- We clamour for attention to our needs but are often unfeeling toward the needs of others in our world.
- We are lenient with our own faults but severe with the faults of others.
- We are weak when things go poorly and self-satisfied when they go well.
- We are quick to speak and slow to listen.
- We often judge on outward appearances before discovering the character within others.

We ask that you be patient with us and continue assisting us in crafting our souls and values. Forgive us our foolish and selfish ways. Be patient when we slip and falter. Lead us onward in moments of despair and disequilibrium. Above all make us ever aware that you extend your great graciousness and love to us. Make us also aware that we cannot pray and acknowledge your presence without also bringing with us all of your other children of this world. They stand with us this day. Help us embrace them in our concern: our sisters and brothers in Christ; the wayward and the hateful; the broken and the lost; the warring and destructive, even our enemies; the suffering and the defeated.

Help us to make room in our hearts for all your children, however unattractive they may be to us. Help us to be loving people and make room in our hearts for all. And cause us to reach out and to find that special task to which you would call each of us. Amen

Fifth Sunday in Lent	Ezekiel 37:1-14	Psalm 130
March 13, 2005	Romans 8:6-11	**John 11:1-45**

Our gracious and eternal God, we thank you for the splendour of the earth about us and for your beautiful creation.

- We thank you for the brilliant sun and clear blue skies.
- We thank you for the lake country and hills through which we walk and drive and which constantly impress us with your splendour.
- We thank you for the return of springtime, color and hope.

Gracious God, compassionate and caring, we thank you that our sufferings are not undergone apart from your watchful eye and care. We thank you that you know when we hurt. We thank you that Jesus walked with those who went through difficult valleys. We thank you that he cared for those who grieved and was touched by their sorrow when he awakened Lazarus.

We need your assistance with us on our life journeys. Be with each of us when we walk through the darkness. Be with each of us as we seek to keep our lives in perspective. Be with us; teach us the art of humility.

- Help us always to see you as the source of all our blessings and to resist the pride of thinking our successes are only due to our own ingenuity.
- Help us to affirm our gifts but save us from thinking, or conveying to others, that our gifts are a cut above others.
- Help us, most of all, to be protected from our vain selves.
- Help us always to elevate others and never to put them down.
- And help us to see ourselves as, and always attempt to be, your faithful servants.

Be with the suffering, the discouraged, the lonely, the depressed, the grieving. Amen

O eternal God, like those early folk who lined the road into Jerusalem as Jesus passed by we too are guilty of holding the wrong hopes and expectations from him.

- They wanted a warrior. We too idolize and place our trust in warriors and superior and sophisticated weaponry.
- They wanted a political solution where Jesus would take power. We too want to trust more in might and in power.
- They wanted revenge. We too often inwardly want and crave for revenge.
- They identified their oppressors as evil. We too are inclined toward the simplistic and we want to divide up the world into good and evil people.

Gentle Jesus, parade yourself again on this Palm Sunday. And do not pass by but stay and invade the inward citadels of our souls with your ways.

- Correct us where we go astray.
- Assist us with the almost impossible human task of loving the unlovable which includes our enemies.
- Help us to learn how to transcend the differences we have and to learn the art of reconciliation and forgiveness.
- Bring peace to our souls, O Prince of Peace!

Make us a part of a great Christian force which brings healing of the human spirit and joy and laughter to our broken world. Help us not to use our faith to build walls, to condemn anyone in your human family, to support our wars or our politics, or to set us apart from others. Instead may we be made more aware of our identification and bond with all of your children.

For those who suffer and mourn we ask your care. For our divided world we ask for a vision among its leaders to work for peace and reconciliation. Amen

Eternal God, we bow before you in awe this Easter day. We bow because of a mystery beyond our comprehension. Twenty centuries later we are as much novices about the resurrection as were those early witnesses. We are as much in need of Jesus' words, "Peace be still" as were his disciples. We thank you that he left word that he would go before them to Galilee and he goes before us.

- He goes before us to the places where we have fears and anxious feelings.
- He goes before us to the places where we feel vulnerable and threatened.
- He goes before us to the places to which we are called but which we feel afraid to venture.
- He goes before us to the places where we humanly posture and compete for positions of honor and privilege.

We thank you that you know our human failings and still call us, nurture us, and lead us. Remake us and make us victorious people. Make us receptive to growth and mastery of life and assist us to overcome the world. Make us resurrection people who are able to dream bigger dreams and able to make this a better world.

Be with those who struggle with illness, disability, grief and transitions not of their own making. Grant comfort, courage, and strength to them. Be also with those who suffer from war, ancient hatreds, terror, and all other forms of inhumanity to others. We find it hard to pray for the perpetrators of violence because it stirs up so much anger, frustration, and hatred within us. But pray for them we must. So be with our enemies and all who are hard of heart. Bring your world to a resurrection of peace. Give us courage to trust in love rather than force, persuasion rather than coercion. Amen

Eternal God, we come before you a bit shaky some days. The world is so much with us that we lose our focus and our center. We become obsessed with cares and concerns. We witness continued rancorous behaviour among our politicians. Our attentions become scattered, our perspective skewed, and our vision diminished. Come to us and heal us.

- Heal us, so that where we have lost our way or where we have compromised our integrity you might restore us to better behaviour.
- Heal us, so that when we lose ourselves in rage over that which cannot be controlled we learn to let go and come to a quiet acceptance.
- Heal us, so that when we lose sight of whose we are we may know once again that we are embraced by you in Jesus the Christ.
- Heal us, so that when we feel alienated from others we may reach out to embrace, and be embraced by, your Christian community and know we have a spiritual home with our fellow seekers.
- Heal us, so that when we fail to fulfill the mission to which you have called us we may be refocused on those values and treasures which are eternal.

In times of joy may we rejoice. In times of sorrow and pain for others may we support and reach out to them and offer support. In times of conflict may we be understanding. We pray that you will guide us as we make our claims on today and tomorrow. May we have long arms with a long reach to include the least of your children throughout the earth.   Amen

Our gracious, eternal God, like these two on the Emaus Road we frequently walk along our roads of life in despair and without hope.

- Like them we walk in sadness.
- Like them we are impatient with those who do not understand life and events as we do.
- Like them we reel and allow ourselves to be set back by disappointments.
- Like them we fail to see the Jesus who would walk along with us.
- Like them we too readily see evil triumph over good and think that is the last word.
- And like them we too quickly and too easily succumb to hopelessness.

Forgive us our foolishness and resurrect our spirits so that we may we see you in the breaking of bread, so that we may we see you in our neighbours, and so that we may we see you in the events of history and the events of each day.

Remove our blindness so that our eyes may be opened and our spirits renewed and our minds astounded. Send us scurrying to the Christian community to share our testimony, to tell of your power, to be renewed by the witness and confirmation of the stories of others. Then fill us all, O Jesus, with your words: "Peace be still," and send us forth confidently to serve this world.

We pray also for our world. Where there is conflict bring peace. Where there is uncertainty and anxiousness bring inner quiet. Where there is hatred bring understanding and love. Where there is the terror of war hover over your earth and bring a change to people's hearts. Where there is selfishness bring generosity and a change of heart. Where there is peril bring comfort and courage. Amen

Fourth Sunday of Easter <u>Acts 2:42-47</u>   Psalm 23

April 17, 2005   I Peter 2:19-25   John 10:1-10

O holy One, we come thankful for a new day. We thank you for the coming of spring-like weather and the hope of having winter behind us. We thank you for the gentle skies and warmer temperatures which also moderate our spirits.

We also thank you for those venturous folk who so long ago encountered Jesus and risked their all.

- We thank you that they did not devalue their potential in spite of their fears.
- We thank you that they saw hope in community and were willing to sacrifice for one another.
- We thank you that they had the courage to put themselves to your service.
- We thank you that they broke bread with glad and generous hearts.
- And we thank you that they trusted you to increase their numbers.

We pray that we might have their kind of courage and trust. We pray that we might be willing to sacrifice for the needs of others. Help us to learn the lessons they would still teach us as their engagement with their world reverberates through the centuries and still is challenging today. Instil within us the same restless stirrings which will cause us anew to consider our purpose and vision. And cause us to have their contagious excitement about our faith.

Be with all this day who have special needs. For those living with the emptiness of grief we ask a sense of your companionship. May they know the tenderness of Jesus as he wept over a friend who died. Be with our friends who are away or travelling. Be with those facing changes in their lives and all who need strength for tomorrow. Amen

Our gracious, eternal God, we are blessed to live in a land of religious freedom. We have never had to experience our faith under the fire of persecution as did Stephen. We are grateful for that. But we also ask that you help us to be faithful in this generation. We ask your blessing upon the church in our time and in all places.

- Give it conviction and a certainty of faith but save it from a crippling over-zealousness.
- Give it zeal but save it from a rigidity which is exclusive and judgmental and which fails to respect those whose faith is different but equally followed.
- Give it truth but save it from the rigidity of an orthodoxy which enslaves and has not the grace to be inclusive.
- Give it civic responsibility but save it from imposing its agenda upon others.
- Give it a commitment to values but save it from imposing narrow values upon others.

Above all give us love and the grace to be open to all peoples, to have the receptive grace of Jesus, to reach out to the lost and the suffering, to know the grace of a forgiving heart, and to be your servant to all forms of human brokenness. Make of us, and make of the church everywhere, communities which are noted for care, committed in faith, and contagious in enthusiasm.

In our world where we see religion in which zeal and anger have overcome grace and compassion we ask your healing. Be with the churches and the nations, O God. Teach us that there are no righteous wars, only groups or nations which have gone astray. Teach us to learn to love and to forgive and to love our enemies. And teach the nations to seek justice and equity. Amen

Our gracious, eternal God, as we reflect upon our modern life we almost feel as if we are in Athens and Paul is speaking to us again. We live in a world where there is considerable talk about spirituality. Yet we are confused about the meaning of our religious symbols. We are divided both between and among what ought to be the same Christian faith, to say nothing of other world religions. As we build cathedrals of belief that wall out others we refuse to listen to or to hear or to give credibility to the integrity within other belief systems. We need your saving help on our journey.

- Save us from our narrowness.
- Save us from the confusion of our minds.
- Save us from a wandering tentativeness and lead us to a convinced and committed faith.
- Save us from searching for unknown gods and lead us to know you whom Paul proclaimed that day in the Areopagus.
- Above all save us from trying to define you who are the creator, who are from everlasting to everlasting, and to make you too small. May we see you in the majesty of your creation, in the beautiful surrounding lakes, in the act of a mother wood duck coaxing her brood out of their home and into the water, in all acts of human kindness, and in the majesty of your love and care.

We pray for those who continue in harms way: for those who are in our military and far from home, for those weekend warriors who have had their lives interrupted by a surprise recall to active duty, for those maimed in war, for those in daily danger. Especially be with those who are called to dangerous missions and who carry out what is always the brutality of war. Be with the innocent. Be with our enemies. Amen

24

Seventh Sunday of Easter
or Ascension Day   **Acts 1:6-14**   Psalm 68:1-10, 32-35
May 8, 2005   I Peter 4:12-14, 5:6-11   John 17:1-11

Eternal God, we bow with gratitude on this Mother's Day and Festival of the Christian Home. We give you our deepest thanks for so many blessings.

- We thank you for the nurture which was ours in our homes and families.
- We thank you for parents who helped shape within us a vision for life and a heavenly vision.
- We thank you for families which, though sometimes struggling, continue to work faithfully to create a safe and loving environment for their children.
- We thank you for children and grandchildren who continue to bring us joy, who teach us to see things in life we would otherwise hurriedly pass by, and who with their freshness and spontaneity remind us that life is an interesting and exciting enterprise.

Enable us to provide children and their families support, care, and direction. May we receive each one as one of your "little ones," Lord Jesus, to whom you so gently bid a welcoming "come unto me."

We pray also for families which are less traditional. Be with those who are single parents. Be with those of the same gender. Be with those who are multigenerational. Be with those who are working hard to believe in their children and to bring them to belief. Be with those who are trying to instil in their children a vision of a moral and Christian life. Wherever they are trying to give them a vision for a better world and a sense of responsibility in working for the larger kingdom we ask that you give blessing. We pray also for families less fortunate where a pattern of abuse has been the only coping path available for the frustrated. Bring to them healing, hope and a vision of a better life and world. Amen

O gentle Spirit, on this Pentecost Sunday we ask that you woo us once again from the falseness of our human foolishness.

- Woo us from our tendency to build walls between our sisters and brothers and bring us unity of heart and understanding like that first Pentecost day.
- Woo us from the divisiveness and confusion of all that is symbolized by Babylon and lead us to receive and to understand others' truths.
- Woo us from ever thinking that war can ever be a real solution to the differences of the world.
- Woo us to wish for, and to work for, peace and justice among all of your peoples.
- Woo us as nations to correct the injustices which lead to such a clearly defined map in our world where poverty and terrorism live hand in hand.

We are grateful, O God, for those who have gone before us and carried the tradition of the Spirit forward: for those who have been able to dream distant dreams; for those whose visions can always see light however much darkness there seems to be; for those who teach us that life always leans forward and that to clutch too closely to the past is always a destructive posture.

On this great Pentecost day renew our spirits. If any be walking through dark valleys point them to the mountaintops. If any be facing difficulty grant them strength, certainty, and your gentle presence. If any be facing transitions lead them firmly forward.

Be with the physically needy. Comfort the grieving, especially in those moments of intense emptiness when life seems as if it will never have quality again. Bless our world and bring hope to those in danger. Amen

O Eternal One, the biblical descriptions of your majestic creative work in calling this world into being create in us a sense of reverence, awe, and great mystery. The ancient people's journey from understanding you as a tribal, territorial, limited deity to understanding you as the creative God of all the universe was punctuated with much suffering, struggle, questioning, anxiety, and then finally a larger vision. By the waters of Babylon the prophet challenged his people for their small and limited vision of God:

"Have you not known? Have you not heard?
The Lord is the everlasting God, the
          creator of the ends of the earth.
He does not faint or grow weary;
          his understanding is unsearchable.
He gives power to the faint,
          and strengthens the powerless." Is. 40:28

It is almost beyond our comprehension that you, the Creator of all, should also care for each of us in times when our power is faint. Yet we find comfort in those words of Isaiah "…that we shall run and not be weary, we shall walk but not faint." Help us to trust and save us from those times when our concept of you is too small.

- May we bow before the mystery of your creative power.
- May we never fail to see the beauty of your creation because we pass through life hurriedly.
- May we, having seen glimpses of the vastness of space which were denied to the ancient folk, never fail to have a sense of wonder and awe and appreciation for your creative handiwork.
- May we always stop to consider the "lilies of the field" and the glory and beauty of creation.
- May we also be good caretakers of the environment of nature which we have inherited. Amen

Our gracious, eternal God, we bow on a beautiful morning with adoration, wonder, and awe. We experience great wonder whenever we ponder life. We are amazed that somehow in the vastness of human history, somehow in the vastness of the universe, somehow in the vastness of the human genetic pool with its myriad possibilities, somehow you have seen fit to call each one of us in our uniqueness into being. You call us by name, you love us with an everlasting love, and you place us within this faithful community. We are reminded powerfully of the Psalmist's confession that we are fearfully and wonderfully made. And we bow again in wonder over your creative love.

We need your help on our Christian journey. We do not wish to be people who call on you on Sunday and forget you on Monday. We need congruence in our Christian walk. While our Christian walk will never approximate our talk help us daily to make it more so. Help us to be doers of your will. Help us to build our lives on a solid rock and a firm foundation.

- Teach us to respond to your love so that we may in turn love you with all our hearts, minds, souls, and strength.
- Teach us to walk lovingly with our brothers and sisters.
- Teach us always to remember that you love others even as you love us.
- Teach us to learn behaviours which demonstrate love and honour for all. Teach us sensitivity to others needs and hurts.

Where our vision of ministry is too small stretch our souls. Make us effective instruments for outreach, for ministries of compassion, and for hospitality and embrace for those who are our guests. May we welcome all in the name of our welcoming Jesus. Amen

Proper 5 (10)   Genesis 12:1-9   Psalm 33:1-12 or *Hosea 5:15-6:6*
June 5, 2005   Psalm 50:7-15   Romans 4:13-25
                    Matthew 9:9-13, 18-26

Our gracious, eternal God, we are reminded this day of so much that is ungracious in our collective religious unconscious. When Jesus called Matthew and ate with sinners he set off an emotional firestorm.

- He provoked feelings of disgust.
- He provoked feelings of anger.
- He provoked feelings of distrust.
- He provoked feelings of resentment.
- He provoked feelings of betrayal of the favouritism which the folk around him thought was their due.
- He provoked strong feelings of disappointment.

They were not prepared for, or willing to accept, or to receive, Jesus' statement of grace that "Those who are well have no need of a physician, but those who are sick."   Unfortunately we are not unlike those angry folk.

- Like them we so easily get caught up in thinking how bad others are.
- Like them we get entrapped by the trappings of our faith and lose its central truth of grace.
- Like them we long for special privilege.
- Like them we think we should be rewarded for our grand religious performances.
- And like them we are reluctant to make room for the sinners and the lost and find it easier to push them away.

Save, us gracious God, from this destructive behaviour. Redeem us once again. Grow our souls large that we might make room for those who struggle, those who stray, and those who have lost their way. Help us to withhold our judgment which is often so harsh. And help to embrace each of your children you present to us. Amen

29

Proper 6 (11)   Genesis 18:1-15, (21:1-7)   Psalm 116:1-2, 12-19 or
June 12, 2005   *Exodus 19:2-8a*   Psalm 100   Romans 5:1-8
Matthew 9:35-10:8, (9-23)

Our gracious, eternal God, we bow this day aware of how much
we need your compassion.

- We come before you sometimes with little expectation
  because of the "dry and weary land" nature of our lives
  at those moments.
- We come before you sometimes as did the crowds,
  harassed, under stress, wondering how we will meet the
  demands about us.
- We come before you sometimes with little confidence in
  our own adequacy to meet the expectations placed upon
  us.
- We come before you sometimes feeling like helpless
  children.
- We come before you sometimes as did that crowd feeling
  like sheep without a shepherd.
- We come before you sometimes in such personal confusion
  that we find the call to be your labourers to the world
  daunting and impossible.

We ask for your compassion anew. Brace up our faltering wills. Help
us less to rely upon ourselves and more to rely upon and to place our
trust in you and your strength. Give us courage in the face of a vision
which seems impossible. Give us the fortitude to rise to the serious
challenge of being your servant people. Give us authority to confront
the demons of our age and to present the message of the holy one
Jesus to the world. In the process we pray that you would help us rid
from our souls all haughtiness, false pride, and all of our tendencies
to draw circles which are too small and shut others out. Expand our
ability to love others by your great love demonstrated in the cross of
Jesus where you have met and embraced all the earth. Amen

Proper 7 (12)   Genesis 21:8 21   Psalm 86:1-10 or *Jeremiah 20:7-13*
June 19, 2005   Romans 6:1b-11   **Matthew 10:24-39**

Eternal God, we thank you for each new day you grant to us. Help us always to remember that it is you who have bestowed life upon us and it is to you to whom we give appropriate thanks. Help us in those moments when we take life for granted or when we have a tendency to grumble and complain. Remind us then of whose we are. We ask not to be reminded harshly, but to be reminded to pause and thank you.

- Remind us to thank you for all of your blessings and your mercies to us.
- Remind us to thank you for our dear ones.
- Remind us to thank you for the Christian community and our sisters and brothers in Christ.
- Remind us to thank you for a glorious and spectacular creation here in our lake and hill country which daily cause us to pause, to behold, and to give praise.
- Remind us to thank you for those who provide us encouragement and vision.

Be with us in our journey as we seek to give serious heed to the words and teachings of Jesus. When fear would paralyze us give us the ability somehow to trust you, to know that we are of more value than the sparrows which are also under your watchful eye. When loyalties would divide us give us the ability to be like Jesus, the teacher and master. Help us to be his followers. Give us the ability to put aside our selfish desires and to commit ourselves and lose ourselves in the centuries old cause of Jesus

O God, there are those who find it difficult to be thankful because they are overwhelmed by the pains and anguish of their journey. Be a strong presence for them. Hold them gently and tenderly in your love and give them strength when theirs seems to be exhausted. Be also in all those places of the earth where folk suffer and use the resources of the Christian community in binding up their wounds. Amen

Proper 8 (13)   Genesis 22:1-14   Psalm 13 or *Jeremiah 28:5-9*
June 26, 2005   Romans 6:12-23   **Matthew 10:40-42**

O Eternal one, we thank you for the record of the biblical witness which documents your love affair with our humankind. We thank you for these words of Jesus which remind us of our need to be welcoming. We thank you that you continually stretch us to reach beyond ourselves.

- Stretch us to widen our souls to include others of your children whom we might naturally exclude.
- Stretch us to grasp for more than we can reach.
- Stretch us to believe in ourselves and others.
- Stretch us to support and encourage others.
- Stretch us to offer a cup of cold water, food, shelter and a safe-haven in your name.

We pray that we might learn the lessons of Christian community. Help us to be instructed by the errors of the past in order that we may be saved from repeating them. Help us to learn exciting new behaviours and new ways. Temper our penchant for holding resentments.

- Teach us that life does not have to be marred permanently by resentments.
- Teach us that life is much more positive and meaningful and satisfying when it is focused on love.
- Teach us that forgiveness is not a sign of weakness but of strength.
- Teach us to build more expansive souls which can reach out and embrace the least of your little ones.

Send your peace and love and overwhelm and transform all of the bitterness and anger which we so often want to hold close to our souls. So lead us in your higher way.

For all who suffer and need your special grace we lift up our prayers today. Amen

Proper 9 (14)   Genesis 24:34-38, 42-49, 58-67   Psalm 45:10-17 or
July 3, 2005   *Song of Solomon 2:8-13* or   *Zechariah 9:9-12*
          Psalm 145:8-14   Romans 6:15-25a
          Matthew 11:16-19, 25-30

Eternal God, we thank you that we have been planted in this great land. We could have been born in the third world somewhere with little opportunity either to learn or to dream or to live beyond childhood. We are grateful for our country. May our actions as a people be congruent with what we with our lips profess. We have been among the most privileged people in all of history. Many of our public places have engraved the powerful words: "The truth shall make you free." And in one of our hymns we claim you as "Our Father's God...Author of Liberty, to thee we sing."

Yet we have been a land which has known slavery and terrible cruelty and we still bear the scars from generation to generation. Many are still disenfranchised from an equal opportunity for a quality education and employment. O God, may we never forget to proclaim: "From every mountainside, let freedom ring." May all be granted a place at the table of opportunity. Give us courage to work for that ideal.

Having been blest with the most lavish bounties the earth has ever known may we never forget to care for the least of those among us. May we provide open doors for the disadvantaged, protection and care for the handicapped, and sharing of our resources with those who are disenfranchised from our economic abundance.

Teach us generosity and save us from the greed and avarice which so punctuates our economic and corporate world. Save us all from the darkness and deviousness to which we are so easily inclined, in order that:

"Long may our land be bright,
With freedom's holy light."

Lead us, O God, to reach for the highest and best in our national life. Amen

Proper 10 (15) Genesis 25:19-34 Psalm 119:105-112 or *Isaiah 55:10-13*
July 10, 2005   Psalm 65:(1-8), 9-13   Romans 8:1-11
Matthew 13:1-9, 18-23

Our gracious eternal God, we thank you for making the earth produce in such abundance. We thank you for the warm gentle summer days, for beautiful lakes, for the warm sun and the cool water, for the restoring rains. We thank you for those who have been toiling to produce the nation's food. And we thank you for the abundance of conveniences which allow us time, in this generation, for considerable leisure and the pursuit of interests other than work.

We pray that you would guide us on our journeys through this land of such abundance. Help us not to be seduced into thinking that material resources can ever make us happy or content. Help us as we see our neighbours' success not to feel inadequate, deprived, or greedy. Help us rather to find our strength, our comfort, and our satisfaction in knowing whose we are and to live life with a sense of peace. Provide us an inner serenity which exterior things can never bring.

We are reminded by the parable of the sower that we carry a huge responsibility for spreading the good news in our time. Give us eyes to see and ears to hear.

- Purge our souls of the rocky ground where your seed cannot grow.
- Purge our souls of the thorns and thistles and of the distractions of life which would lure us to fleeting and competing treasures.
- Purge our souls of the wish to build storehouses with the elusive hope of ridding ourselves of anxiety about the future.

Make us grow from the kind of soil which knows the value of commitment, the risk of trust, and the mystery of your grace and love. Amen

Proper 11 (16)   Genesis 28:10-19a Psalm 139:1-12, 23-24 or *Wisdom of*
July 17, 2005 *Solomon 12:13, 16-19 or Isaiah 44:6-8* Psalm 86:11-17
             Romans 8:12-25   Matthew 13:24-30, 36-43

Our gracious, eternal God, we come before you with gratitude
this day.

- We are grateful that we are a part of a long and struggling,
  yet victorious community.
- We are grateful that the upward path of your realm, always
  beset with obstacles and difficulties, nonetheless remains
  our vision.
- We are grateful that life, while stained with imperfections,
  yet can be ennobled by those who persist and persevere.
- We are grateful with St. Paul that we did not receive
  a "spirit of slavery to fall back into fear, but (we) have
  received a spirit of adoption."
- And we are grateful that we have received a spirit of
  freedom and grace to know that we are indeed your
  children.

We pray that you will continue to provide correction for us when
we miss the mark. We pray that we may be stretched to learn and
to grow. We pray that we might be enabled to grow bigger, more
generous, more inclusive, and more loving hearts. Help us to affirm
one another and to build up and embrace the gifts among us.

We also pray for our world.   Beset with wars, conflicts, famine,
corruption, domination by the powerful, suffering of the weak, there
hardly seems a time in which your creation has been groaning with
such travail as it is now. Where there is conflict, bring peace. Where
there is suffering bring healing and compassion. Where there is
uncertainty and anxiousness bring inner peace. Where there is hatred
and enmity bring understanding and unity and love. Amen

Proper 12 (17) Genesis 29:15-28 Psalm 105:1-11, 45b or Psalm 128
July 24, 2005 or I Kings 3:5-12 Psalm 119:129-136
Romans 8:26-39 Matthew 13:31-33, 44-52

O Eternal One, whatever our attitude is as we bow today, whether upbeat or depressed, we are comforted by those stirring words of St. Paul that "If God is for us, who is against us?" We thank you for this breakthrough in our human understanding of you which put behind us the concept of a punitive God. We thank you for all of the gentle reminders of how much you love us. Whenever we become anxious in our souls we pray that you would remind us that you are still in charge of the universe. Provide us with an inner serenity which outward circumstances cannot shake. Remind us to use the treasures of earth to meet our needs but may we never confuse them with the treasures of the eternal.

WALK WITH US IN THE UPS AND DOWNS OF LIFE.

- Grant to those who are sad, comfort.
- Grant to those who feel weak, strength.
- Grant to the strong and confident, understanding and compassion.
- Grant to the successful, humility.
- Grant to those experiencing doubt, faith.
- Grant to those facing a critical decision, wisdom and guidance.
- Grant to the confused, clarity of purpose.
- Grant to those whose hold on life is tenuous, the comfort of Jesus who does not condemn but who justifies and receives with such gentle grace.

Whatever our circumstance, give to all of us the confidence that we are "more than conquerors," so that when the great call comes we know with assurance that "nothing in all creation will be able to separate us from the love of God which is in Christ Jesus our Lord." Amen

36

Proper 13 (18) Genesis 32:22 31   Psalm 17:1-7, 15 or Isaiah 55:1-5
July 31, 2005   Psalm 145:8-9, 14-21   Romans 9:1-5
                          Matthew 14:13-21

Our gracious, eternal God, we bow and acknowledge how near you are to us.

- You are nearer than our thoughts but beyond our thoughts and unable to be grasped completely by thought or concept however hard we try.
- You are enshrouded in mystery yet you invite us to speak to you as a loving parent.
- You invite us to seek that we might find, yet we have been found and embraced by you before we even venture forth.

We thank you for your love and graciousness to us. Teach us as Jesus instructed his disciples of old. Like them we seek retreat and quiet for ourselves but we ask that you teach us when to step forward with boldness and trust. Teach us not to minimize the resources you have given us but to know that when we move at your command you will multiply our scant resources and make them not only adequate but plenty. Like those who offered the loaves and fishes help us to offer what we have in the service of your children.

Lead us gently but steadily toward the heavenly vision. Making no claims for ourselves may we ever know that we have been claimed by you in your son Jesus.

We pray for our world, groaning with travail, war and suffering. Be with those who must carry out the horrors of war and who live with the scars of what they see daily and what they are called upon to do. Be with the innocent victims. Be with the maimed, the suffering, the grieving. We pray again that you would lead us to peace. And lead the nations of the earth and help them find better ways of resolving conflict. Amen

Proper 14 (19) Genesis 37:1-4, 12-28 Psalm 105:1-6, 16-22, 45b or

August 7, 2005 I Kings 19:9-18   Psalm 85:8-13

                Romans 10:5-15   **Matthew 14:22-33**

Eternal One, we thank you that we can pause and worship on a day like this. We thank you for the freedom we have to worship.

- Forgive us our ambivalence when we turn that freedom into a gnawing guilt-ridden exercise which brings us to worship but only reluctantly.
- Forgive us our tendency to complain that this, your world, is not a better place due to humankind's sinfulness.
- Forgive us our tendency to be complacent and expect someone else to make improvements when we are unwilling to be involved.
- Forgive us our inability to trust in you when the cares of the world rise up before us and cause us to fear and to cower.

Be to us a powerful, healing presence when our fears and anxieties become overwhelming. Like Peter when he was sinking we too sometimes feel like we are sinking and overwhelmed by life. We look at the storm around us, and sometimes the storm within us, and our fears intensify. Be the source of our strength when we are weak. Be a solid rock beneath our feet when we wander and when we falter and slip. Be our shield and wrap your protective arms around us when we face danger and cause the wind and the storms of life within to be calmed.

Be with those whose walk is lonely. Be with those who have been forced to go off to war. Be with those who are in danger daily. Be with the hungry and the destitute and the homeless. Give us the grace and the vision to craft a new world where all of your children eat at a table of plenty, where all are sheltered, and where peace and love and justice abound. Amen

Proper 15 (20)   Genesis 45:1-15   Psalm 133 or *Isaiah 56:1, 6-8*   Psalm 67
August 14, 2005   Romans 11:1-2a, 29-32   **Matthew 15:(10-20), 21-28**

Our gracious, eternal God, on this Lord's day we join with the
ancient hymn of the Psalm writer:
"May God be gracious to us and bless us,
And make his face to shine upon us."
We join further in praise with that same ancient hymn:
"Let the peoples praise you O God;
Let all the peoples praise you."
As your people we are grateful that when we behold the world, even
when times are difficult, we find more than ample reason to express
our gratitude.
- We are grateful for our magnificent creation.
- We are grateful for the majesty of the mountains.
- We are grateful for the vastness and beauty of the oceans
  and the varied but always beautiful coastal areas.
- We are grateful for thick, tall forests.
- We are grateful for the diversity of people and the diversity
  of their gifts.
- We are grateful for the splendour of beautiful sunsets.
- We are grateful for family and friends and a Christian
  community to receive us.
We are of all people most richly blessed. Let us praise you, O God,
let all of us praise you.
   Yet there are so many in our world whose journeys provide little
hope. Be with those whose cities and countries are punctuated with
bullets, bombs, and terror. Be with those for whom there is no justice
and equity. Be with those who suffer innocently at the hand of brutal
governments or systems. Be also with the homeless and the helpless;
the ill and the indigent; the discouraged and the despondent; the lost
and the lonely. Amen

39

Proper 16 (21)   Exodus 1:8 – 2:10   Psalm 124 or *Isaiah 51:1-6*
August 21, 2005   Psalm 138   **Romans 12:1-8**   Matthew 16:13-20

Our gracious, eternal God, we thank you this day for the instruction of scripture. Paul reminds us of our human struggle for self worth and a positive self image. Yet in that struggle how quickly we become vulnerable to thinking more highly of ourselves than we ought. We know that we succumb to false pride. We know that the other side of false pride is that we really are feeling poorly about ourselves. Yet how often we lose our way and lose perspective. We confess that in this competitive society of ours we want to rise above others. Lend us sober judgment.

- Remind us that we were made for community.
- Remind us that we are meant to walk with our sisters and brothers in the faith.
- Remind us to set forth our views to others but not to insist always on our own way.
- Remind us not to minimize our own gifts but to present them for the betterment of the Christian community.
- Remind us to tease forth and bless the gifts of others.
- Remind us that we are all one body of Christ and members one of another.

In all things make us compassionate. In all things continue to transform us and to renew our minds, hearts, and spirits so that we may truly discern your will and your ways.

We pray for our world. We have witnessed so much brutality these past years. We pray that you would implant within the hearts of all your creatures the desire to diminish the inhumanity to others which is so prevalent in our broken world. Bring peace. But also bring peaceful and loving hearts.

We would also breathe a prayer for those who must walk through the valley of suffering. Bring them healing and hope. Amen

Proper 17 (22)   Exodus 3:1-15   Psalm 105:1-6, 23-26, 45c or
August 28, 2005   *Jeremiah 15:15-21*   Psalm 26:1-8 **Romans   12:9-21**
                    Matthew 16:21-28

Eternal God, we bow with thankful hearts today. We have been blessed with a gentle summer and consistent rains. Those who raise our nations' food have had a good growing season. The mountains have been wonderfully green and the rivers and streams have been full and clear. The beauty around us has been spectacular. We are so blessed and we thank you.

We give thanks today for Paul's pep talk to the church which was in Rome. But we also struggle because we need your help in the ups and downs of our lives.

- Help us to love more completely and to control the ever-present tendency to give in to hatred.
- Help us to show honour to others and not to have resentment or envy when they do well.
- Help us when we grow weary and feel defeated to find new zeal and ardour on our Christian journey.
- Help us to maintain a hopeful attitude and a hopeful spirit even when life takes a difficult turn.
- Help us especially when we are called upon to go through the valley of suffering, when the "why?" questions surface our anger.
- Help us to find the empathy and compassion needed to rejoice with those who rejoice and to weep with those who weep.
- Help us not to think we are better than others but enable us to relate to and be genuine with people at all levels of our society.
- And help us not to return evil for evil even when we would most wish to get even with another person. Amen

Our gracious, eternal God, we sometimes feel too much like a work in progress and wonder if we are not really making false starts. We have much to confess.

- We poison relationships with others by drawing faulty conclusions from our limited perceptions.
- We nurture slights even though we are far from sure a slight has occurred.
- We find it easier to blame others when a relationship becomes strained rather than looking to our role in the cause.
- We find it so much easier to think we have been sinned against than to think that we are the ones who have sinned.
- We find it easier to nurture a wrong when it is committed against us than to go directly to the person and surface the issue openly.
- And we find it difficult to admit our own wrongs and ask another for forgiveness.

Forgive us our foolish ways, O gracious, loving, God.

- Give us the courage both to forgive and to ask forgiveness.
- Give us confidence in the integrity of others to trust that they too wish to walk in a covenanted relationship with us.
- Give us the courage to deepen relationships by keeping them honest and open.
- Give us the courage to heed the ancient words we have heard today and go to the other person directly to clear the air and heal the relationship when we feel we have been wronged. Amen

Proper 19 (24)   Exodus 14:19-31   Psalm 114 or *Exodus 15:1b-11, 20-21* or
September 11, 2005   *Genesis 50:15-21*   Psalm 103: (1-7), 8-13
                    Romans 14:1-12   **Matthew 18:21-35**

Eternal God, we have learned so little since the ancient wisdom of Israel began to be articulated. You provide for us a way and we turn a deaf ear.

We confess especially on this anniversary of 9/11 that we have not learned the futility of war and violence. We still think we can resolve differences by brute force. We project the worst of motives to our enemies and the best to ours. We continue to demonize our enemies in order to justify killing them. We speak of others as evil but forget or deny the evil which resides in each of us.

Deliver us from this body of death, O God. Save us from refusing to learn. Help us to revise our lives and our culture so that we may gain a heart of wisdom and know you who are the beginning of wisdom. Teach us the difficult spiritual act of learning how to forgive others and to forgive our enemies. Take away from us the calculating spirit of Peter which resides in each one of us and which would measure out forgiveness with a careful and reluctant eye. Transform us, O God.

- Save us from growing weary in the steady and tedious task of keeping relationships cleaned up.
- Save us from trying to set some artificial limits on how far we will go with those who offend us.
- Save us from a calculating faith which tries to put another person outside the Christian circle.
- Save us from being stingy of spirit and denying grace to others.

O God, give us generous and forgiving spirits which make room for the sins and foibles of others. Amen

Proper 20 (25)   Exodus 16:2-15   Psalm 105:1-6, 37-45 or *Jonah 3:10-4:11*
September 18, 2005   Psalm 145:1-8   **Philippians 1:21-30**   Matthew 20:1-16

Eternal God, we open our collective souls to your presence. We come needing to empty ourselves of the baggage and cares of the week and in some cases of life.

- Some have had heavy burdens to bear.
- Some have seen a glimpse of our fragility and mortality and faced the terror and prospect of losing a dear one and come away grateful that they have been spared.
- Some have suffered a disappointment.
- Some have been walking through the dark valleys of the soul and are despondent.
- Some are facing life-changing decisions.
- And many have private worries of their own.

O God, be with us in our common cares and empty us of our worries and anxiousness. Free us from the desire and temptation to clutch and hold close our human treasures. Teach us the wisdom that it is only in losing ourselves in causes and service which transcend ourselves that we truly find ourselves. Help us to cast all our cares upon you, knowing that you love us with an everlasting love. And fill us this day with your peace.

Make us valiant in the service of our world. May we never be discouraged, but as Paul suggested may we be worthy of the gospel of Christ. Even though we will never achieve completely the mission to which you call us we ask for the courage to begin the journey. Enable us to visit the sick, the hurting, the imprisoned. Enable us to care for the least of your children.

Bless our world and bring us peace. Bless our sick and dying and give them hope. Bless our children and give them a gentle and nurturing world. Bless our nation's and world's leaders and give them wisdom and the will to be statesmen. Amen

Proper 21 (26)   Exodus 17:1-7   Psalm 78:1-4, 12-16 or
September 25, 2005   *Ezekiel 18:1-4, 25-32*   Psalm 25:1-9
                       Philippians 2:1-13   Matthew 21:23-32

Eternal God, we thank you that you have placed us within your church. We thank you for the great cloud of witnesses who have gone before us and who carried the lamp of faith to our generation. And we thank you that we now, for a time, have the responsibility to hold it aloft for others. Let the "same mind be in us (you) that was in Christ." Help us to be faithful to the heavenly vision in this place. Give us will and resolve.

- Give us the resolve to put our gifts and talents forward for your use and for others.
- Give us the resolve to support and encourage the gifts of others.
- Give us the resolve to build up a stalwart community with vision and daring and service to our world.
- Give us the resolve to nurture a loving, caring community which reaches out always to the least of your children.
- Give us the resolve to help you put a tap on the shoulder of young people with the gifts to consider some form of ministry.
- Give us the resolve to commit our lives and energy on the side of justice and equity for all of the peoples of the earth.
- Give us the resolve to right the wrongs and the discrimination of the past and to transcend prejudice and racism.
- And give us the resolve to be a people of peace who work for peace.

Cause us to be strong in faith, loyal in service, and patient in hope. Work in us your way, you who are the ageless potter working your clay. Amen

Proper 22 (27) Exodus 20:1-4, 7-9, 12-20 Psalm 19 or *Isaiah 5:1-7*
October 2, 2005 Psalm 80:7-15 **Philippians 3:4b-14**
Matthew 21:33-46

Eternal God, we thank you for this week which has presented us with a panorama of exploding autumn colors. We thank you that you have so painted this world with colors that our eyes almost catch a glow from the brilliance.

We pause on this world-wide communion day, aware of the millions of our sisters and brothers with whom we are united at the table of Jesus Christ. Unite us also in a commitment to service. Bless your people wherever they gather this day in your name. Create unity, love, and Christian witness in each place.

In this great land of so much abundance there are still so many people with great need. In the aftermath of hurricane Katrina people are uprooted, families are separated, a city has been rendered unfit in which to live, other cities and villages have been destroyed. May your church be moved with compassion for all of these "Neighbours in Need." May we who have been spared give generously.

- May we have the vision to give to help the hungry.
- May we have the vision to give to provide an opportunity for a child.
- May we have the vision to give in order to alleviate suffering among the elderly.
- May we have the vision to give to open some doors for those who need opportunity.
- May we have the vision to do all we can to help people rebuild their lives.

May we join St. Paul in "forgetting what lies behind and straining forward to what lies ahead," pressing "on toward the goal for the prize of the heavenly call in Christ Jesus." Amen

Proper 23 (23) Exodus 32:1-14   Psalm 106:1-6, 19-23 or *Isaiah 25:1-9*
October 9, 2005 Psalm 23 **Philippians 4:1-9**   Matthew 22:1-14

O Eternal One, we come before you with grateful hearts this day.

- You have placed us in this beautiful place with hills and valleys which are dotted with lakes outlined by awesome trees.
- You have peopled our lives generously with those who have taught and mentored us and believed in us long before we believed in ourselves.
- You have provided us in this land with an abundance unknown to so many peoples of the earth.

Yet we confess that with such blessings we oftentimes find that the world is heavy and too much with us. Paul admonishes us not to worry but to rejoice. And yet we worry. Our spirits sag and our joy diminishes.

- Give us the resilience of spirit to "rejoice in the Lord always" in spite of the bad news of the world.
- Give us a spirit of gentleness when our rage would rather be unleashed because of the horrific conditions which so many of your children must endure.
- Give us the ability to cast our cares upon you and to present to you the deepest concerns of our hearts.
- Give us your quieting and steadying "peace which passes all understanding."
- Give us joy in the Lord and the gratitude which knows that all our blessings flow from you.

Help us to rejoice in the Lord always! Be also with this congregation and direct our paths. Lead us in being faithful to the heavenly vision. Lead us in deepening our commitments to you and to one another. Lead us in discerning your will among us. Lead us in serving your people. Amen

47

Proper 24 (29)   Exodus 33:12-23   Psalm 99 or *Isaiah 45:1-7*
October 16, 2005   Psalm 96:1-9, (10-13) **I Thessalonians 1:1-10**
    Matthew 22:15-22

Eternal God, we thank you for this day. We are grateful for all that you have granted to us to make our lives full and meaningful.

We confess that we fall short of the Christian walk in so many ways. In our reflections we sometimes wonder if it can be said of us, as it was said of old, that the gospel came to us "not in word only, but also in power and in the Holy Spirit and with full conviction;...." We confess that like the Pharisees we are often inwardly glad that we are not as other people. Whenever we confront one of your children from whom we recoil we demonstrate that we are glad we are not as other people. We need healing, O God.

- We take pride in our righteousness, forgetting that it is you alone who make righteous.
- We take pride in the good things we do, forgetting that our purpose is to glorify you and not ourselves.
- We take pride in what we regard as our good motives and impugn to others the worst of motives.
- We take pride in whatever performances we can give which display our piety but are remiss in developing a private, closet piety where we are alone with you.

Forgive us our sins and failings. Give us the courage to own the sin which so easily besets us and to know once again the power of your grace to embrace and restore us. Likewise give us grace-filled spirits. Cause us to be less condemning of others. Cause us to be less judgmental and to temper our rejecting behaviours. Cause us to be less exclusive and to reach out to all of your children you set in our path. Cause us to be less inclined to build walls between ourselves and others. Cause us to deal with that within us which makes us want to reject any of your children. Cause us to love. Cause us to serve you with power. Amen

Proper 25 (30)	Deuteronomy 34:1-12	Psalm 90:1-6, 13-17 or
October 23, 2005	*Leviticus 19:1-2, 15-18*	Psalm 1
	I Thessalonians 2:1-8	Matthew 22:34-46

Our gracious, eternal God, help us this day to draw our minds and spirits from the hectic confusion of the week. Take our minds from all that would distract us.

- Take from us our cares, our fears, our apprehension about our tomorrows.
- Take from us our resentments, our angers, and all that is negative and destructive, every tendency to want to get even for some perceived wrong.
- Take from us our concerns about earthly treasures and our avaricious desires.
- Take from us our lethargy regarding our spiritual journey.
- Take from us our hatred toward our enemies, however demonically they have acted.
- Take from us all efforts to act deceitfully and to veil the truth from others.

Take our minds from all of this. Help us to focus on your grace which is extended to the greatest of sinners. May we be bathed by your love today, a love which will not let us go. May we be filled with a trust that floods our souls with peace and love. May we be transformed.

Give us leaders with the courage to present the gospel clearly even in the face of opposition. Give them and us integrity as we walk together. Give us a church where there is straight forward communication, where there are no ulterior motives, where there is no false flattery, where there is no greed, where our main motivation is to seek to do your will and not seek the praise of others, where there is mutuality and love. Give us victory and mastery in our common life. Amen

Proper 26 (31)   Joshua 3:7-17   Psalm 107:1-7, 33-37 or
October 30, 2005   *Micah 3:5-12*   Psalm 43
                                    I Thessalonians 2:9-13   Matthew 23:1-12

Our gracious eternal God, we have need to pray this day. We have so much internal confusion and noise and chatter going on all the time. We find ourselves distracted from the good and living the evil.

- We nurture slights and become preoccupied with how ill-willed others often are.
- We hold onto old wrongs which feel like weights on our souls, yet we are reluctant to relinquish them and look for a new start.
- We worry about tomorrow and wonder if you will go before us.
- We draw erroneous conclusions from others' behaviour which are based only on our faulty perceptions.
- And too often we are insistent on our own way.

God, be with us on our journey and walk with us through these internal wars which are so much with us.

- Help us to know that it is our own souls which need re-working.
- Help us to know that it is we who are in need of redemption and reconciliation.
- Help us to know that it is we who are in the need of prayer.
- Help us to try new and more generous behaviours which are filled with love and good will.

O God, transform us and change our defeatist attitudes. Instead of asking for life to be all smooth sailing give us the courage for challenges. Instead of cowering before difficulty give us the strength to embrace it and to overcome. Lead us to be a people of victory, of faith in the future, and of the attitude that with your aid we can overcome the world. Amen

Proper 27 (32)   Joshua 24:1-3a, 14 25   Psalm 78:1-7 or
November 6, 2005   *Wisdom of Solomon 6:12-16* or *Amos 5:18-24*
                         Wisdom of Solomon 6:17-20 or *Psalm 70*
                         I Thessalonians 4:13-18   Matthew 25:1-13

O eternal One, we bow this day in grateful remembrance. Make us resurrection people.

- Make us a people able to dream bigger dreams.
- Make us a people able to make this a better world.
- Make us a people with care and compassion.
- Make us a people who bind up the wounds of the sick, who care enough to feed the poor, who visit the imprisoned.
- Make us a people committed to justice, working for a nation and a world where there is equal opportunity for every person and every child growing up.
- Make us a people who know how to love.

We are particularly mindful on this all saints day that we are surrounded by a great cloud of witnesses. We thank you for our forbears who have enriched our church community by their long ago dreams. We thank you for those who wished to plant a church here. We thank you for those who wished to live the gospel in their time and who cared enough to pass it on to those who would follow. We thank you for those whose faith could see beyond their own time and needs and had hope beyond the grave. We thank you for those who trusted you, the God of our human history. And we thank you for those whose hope could not be diminished by difficulty and hardship. Bless their memory and help us to carry on with the help of that great cloud if witnesses who have gone before us.

Bless the sick and suffering; those whose lives are uprooted; those engaged in war and those suffering from war and violence; those who have special needs.   Amen

51

Proper 28 (33)   Judges 4:1-7 Psalm 123 *or Zephaniah 1:7, 12-18*
November 13, 2005 Psalm 90:1-8, (9-11), 12 **I Thessalonians 5:1-11**
Matthew 25:14-30

Our gracious eternal God, the ancient words of Paul echo in our souls this day. We are so much like the people of the Thessalonian Church and its culture.

- We want to have glimpses of the future so that we might know that we are secure.
- We want to have the security to know that tomorrow will be alright.
- We want to have life all buttoned down and figured out so there will be no surprises.
- We want you to rid us of all anxiety and worry and fear.
- We want to know that when the great call comes for us we will be safe.
- We want all darkness and all uncertainty removed from our lives.

Become alive for us again in these quiet moments. We pray that in this teachable moment you would again open to us your powerful and grace-filled presence.

- Lead our spirits to find the courage to say, "All will be well because we are yours."
- Lead our spirits to find the ability to live one moment and one day at a time.
- Lead our spirits to serenity and a peace which the world cannot give.
- Lead our spirits to know that with your power we can cope with whatever surprises life presents to us.
- Lead our spirits to know that we are destined "not for wrath" but for your redeeming.
- And lead our spirits to know that "whether we wake or sleep," living or dying, we are yours into the ages of all ages. Amen

O eternal one, we come before you with gratitude this Thanksgiving week. Of all people we have been inordinately blessed with bounty and a standard of living which the world has never seen. We have so much for which to be thankful.

- We thank you for plentiful food.
- We thank you for homes which are warm in winter and cool in summer.
- We thank you for an expansive country with stunning beauty.
- We thank you for work and leisure.
- We thank you for family and friends.
- We thank you for a nation built on law which guarantees us religious freedom.

In spite of our blessings we have many concerns. Parts of our country have been ravaged by hurricanes. We are caught in a war which goes on and on and each day brings casualties and tales of sadness and grief. We ask your blessing and care for all who suffer, who have known grief, whose lives are shattered. O divine healer, bring us a better world and bring to the violent restraint. Temper the world's hatreds and bring us peace.

In moments when we would shirk back from the challenges of life to be your people and to reach out and care for others bring an appropriate soberness to our spirits. May we ask: 'When did we see you in the guise of the homeless and fail to help you?' May we ask: 'When did we see you sick or in prison and fail to meet your needs?' May we ask: 'When did we see you as a victim of war or disaster and fail to come to your aid?' May we ask: 'What, O God, do you require of us who have been so blessed?" O God, help us to respond to the Jesus in our neighbour and to serve you. Amen

YEAR B

First Sunday in Advent   **Isaiah 64:1-9**   Psalm 80:1-7, 17-19
November 27, 2005   I Corinthians 1:3-9 Mark 13:24-37

O holy One of Israel, whose long history with your people is punctuated by ups and down, sins and disappointments, transgressions and wanderings, we come before you in humility as we begin our advent journey.

- We confess that like the ancient's our zeal and ardour in being faithful sometimes wanes.
- We confess that we sometimes stray from the best we know.
- We confess that we sometimes sin and fail.
- We confess that we sometimes become insensitive to the needs of our sisters and brothers.
- We confess that we sometimes feel that you are far from us, almost to the point of abandonment.
- We confess that we sometimes feel that you have hidden your face from us.

Help us in these times to continue to make our claim upon you and to know that you have claimed us in Jesus Christ. Help us to know that we are your clay and you are the potter and to know that we are indeed the 'work of your hand.' Help us to know that your anger is not the last word in your relationship with your people. Help us to know that we are indeed your people, and that we will always be, because we have been made so in Jesus who ever comes unto your world.

While we would trust that you are always and ever present may we come to experience that more deeply this advent time. Overcome once again the distance and the uncertainty we have felt on our journey and make us to know your advent peace.

Hover over all those regions of human pain and suffering in our world and bring hope. Amen.

Our gracious, eternal God, give your attention to us as we again seek to "prepare the way of the Lord" on our advent journey.

- When we are weak kneed and world weary lift us up.
- When we have lost our way or lost hope may we hear you speaking softly and tenderly to us.
- When we cannot banish from our minds and continue to hold close the sins of the past give us the courage to claim your grace and to say: "enough is enough."
- When we are fearful of our own mortality give us the trust in your word which endures forever.
- When we are timid or fearful about the message of hope which we proclaim give us the courage to claim and to witness to the good news.

In the midst of all the despair the world and life can present cause us to find comfort in the good news. May we never forget that our message is a message of comfort and of love and of faithfulness.

- Lift us up to a high mountain of living.
- Lift us up to know the power of your might.
- Lift us up to know that you will "feed (your) flock like a shepherd."
- Lift us up to know that you will hold us close to you.
- Lift us up to know that you will gently lead us.

What we pray for ourselves we also pray for others. Be with all those places where inhumanity is shown toward any of your children. Be in those places of war and conflict. Be in the sufferings of those who have experienced natural disasters, persecution or famine. May all the earth be captured by the will to love. May all the earth be touched to change. Amen

Third Sunday of Advent   Isaiah 61:1-4, 8-11   Psalm 126 or
December 11, 2005 *Luke 1:47-55* I Thess. 5:16-24   John 1:6-8, 19-28

Eternal and holy God, nurturing your people in times of trouble and distress, cajoling them in times of ease and apathy, lifting them up in times of despair and depression, creating a new vision in times of plateaus, we come before you on this advent journey needing your mercy and grace.

- Give to us a sense that you have anointed us for the challenges of our day.
- Give us concern for the oppressed and the broken-hearted.
- Give us concern for prisoners and rid us of the desire only to have them put away.
- Give compassion for those who mourn.
- Give us a passion for justice which will not let us rest until all of your children have enough to eat at the table of life.
- Give us a passion for honesty and integrity and save us in our common life from reducing our political life to a pursuit of power and domination.
- Give us a passion for peace and the will to find other ways than war to solve the differences of humankind.

Make us aware of the ways of your child, Jesus, in the living of our days. Make us and mould us, O God, and may we know that you have not finished your work in us. Make us a people who know gratitude, and knowing gratitude know the joy of praise and thanksgiving. Give us a zest for life which puts bounce into our steps and a warm welcome and embrace of each of your children placed in our path.

We ask your care today for those whose health has become vulnerable and for those who are walking through dark valleys. Sustain them and give them hope and courage.   Amen

Fourth Sunday of Advent   2 Sam. 7:1-11, 16   Luke 1:47-55 or
December 18, 2005   *Ps. 89:1-4, 19-26*   Romans 16:25-17
Luke 1:26-38

Our gracious and loving God, we pause during this advent time to give you thanks.

- We thank you for the beautiful stories surrounding the nativity.
- We thank you for the surprise experience of Mary and her receptive spirit which said: "let it be to me according to your word."
- We thank you for the hope which was given in the midst of a culture of despair which stands as a permanent reminder to us that despair often cradles hope.
- We thank you for the promise of your reign which is forever and ever.

During this advent journey may we be overshadowed by your spirit and be changed in our inward hearts.

- May we know that you also walk with us.
- May we know that you care for us and all humankind and though we sometimes give up you never give up on us.
- May we know the joy of a renewed spirit.
- May we know the resolution of will which makes a new commitment and which responds with a willing "Here am I."
- May we know the mystery of your working in and through people.
- And may we know your holy one, Jesus, who became our brother that we might become your children.

We ask your care for our world which is punctuated with so much violence and hatred. Bend low over the twisted hatreds of earth and bring us new life. Melt the hearts of all peoples and bring us peace, O Prince of Peace. Amen

<u>Nativity of the Lord – Proper III</u> Isaiah 52:7-10 Psalm 98
December 24/25, 2005 Heb. 1:1-4, (5-12) **<u>John 1:1-14</u>**

O eternal One, whose light began to shine brightly in Jesus the Christ and whose light continues to illumine all of our earthly darkness, we come before you with thankful hearts during this Christmastide. We thank you that the Word became flesh and that our humanity was blessed because Jesus was full of grace and truth. Bless our celebrations this Christmas and help us to experience again the mystery of your everlasting bonding with your children. Touch us once again with the power of the nativity.

- May we know with Zechariah that you have redeemed your people.
- May we know with the shepherds that the fears and terrors of life are met by the angel who said "Do not to be afraid" and who spoke of good news of great joy.
- May we know with Mary that the mystery of that holy birth will take considerable pondering on our part.
- May we know with Simeon that we have seen your salvation.
- May we know with the Maji to set out on our own religious journeys and finally come to kneel and pay homage to your holy child.

We pray that you would touch us with the best of our religious tradition. Make us open and receptive of all of your children. Take from us all prejudice, pride, and hatred. Take from us all of our tendencies to be harsh in our judgments of others. We ask not that you make loving others easy but we ask for the strength to love. Give us strength to love the hateful. Give us strength to love the enemy. Give us strength to love the broken, the radical, and the prejudiced. Give us strength to put our powers to remaking this, your world. Give us strength to work for peace. Amen

O eternal One, our year now past has been one of so many human tragedies. We have had hurricanes Katrina and Rita brought into our living rooms. We have witnessed many people being killed from war and terror in Iraq and around the world. We have witnessed villages in Pakistan completely flattened by earthquakes. We have witnessed unspeakable tragedy to the point that at times we have felt compassion fatigue where our inmost beings almost cry out: "show me no more!" We pray for those who have endured so much, who have suffered so much, who have lost so much, and who have grieved so much. We pray that by the sheer overwhelming nature of such devastation we may not try to retreat into a protective shell. Open us to our world.

- Open us to the world's suffering to the point that we make a difference in its healing.
- Open us to the destructiveness of war so that we work to make the world a safe and just place for all of its peoples.
- Open us to the needs of the broken of the world and the poor and help us to build societies which provide opportunities for meaningful work so that all may share in the world's bounty.
- Open us to the possibility of accepting and blessing the wonders of the diversity of all peoples and to rise above the prejudices of the past.
- Open us to finding in our religious faiths tolerance and loving behaviours to all of your children.

We do thank you that you have given us a new year. We pray that we may approach it expectantly and with excitement for the opportunities it holds. May we treasure each day. Amen

Our gracious, eternal God, we bow this day thankful for your providential care for us. Through all of the circuitous events of our lives we see the workings of your hand.

- You have given us a sense that you have led us in those times when we have been faced with decisions.
- You have given us hard days to strengthen us.
- You have given us uplifting days of joy to cheer us.
- You have given us difficulties to test and to challenge us.
- You have given us triumphs and victories to celebrate and to enhance our sense of worth and achievement.
- You have given us a sense of community to cope with isolation and loneliness.

As we lean into this new year we ask your blessing. As Jesus became open to baptism so we ask you to lead us to new truth and new decisions. May we take the lessons from the past and lean forward with great expectations for tomorrow. Prevent us from being negative and pessimistic about life.

- May we not repeat the mistakes of the past or languor in them.
- May we not become cynical because our world is not a better place.
- May we not despair over conflict but face it with courage and grace.

Above all may we use whatever uncertainty comes our way to build a stronger faith and trust in you. And may we trust our brothers and sisters on our journey.

Be a strong presence to those with special needs and for all around our beautiful earth who suffer. Amen

O holy One, we thank you for your still small voice which has been heard by your people through the ages. We thank you that you continue to call your people and do not leave any generation without its prophets to proclaim you. When you speak to us and call us help us to respond as did Samuel. Lead us through any confusion until we are able to say: "Speak, LORD, for your servant is listening."

- Help us to listen for your guidance and direction in our lives.
- Help us to listen for the cries of your children who need some response from us.
- Help us to listen to the world around us and to insert our witness and efforts to make our world a better place for all your children.
- Help us to listen to those places where there is inequity and injustice and corruption.
- Help us to listen for your still, small voice prodding us to grow in ways which we most tend to resist.
- Help us to be a listening people so that our faith is not simply a baptizing of our own worldly values and prejudices.
- Help us to listen, O God. Give us courage to say: "Speak, LORD, for your servant is listening."

We pray for your church.   Save it from narrowness and judgmentalism and a divisiveness in which any part of it thinks it possesses and owns the truth. Save it from a destructive partisanship which is unbecoming a people of faith. Save any part of it from rejecting others. May our divisions not prevent us from knowing a oneness in Christ. Save us from rancour and bring us a greater sense of unity. May we see the day when there is oneness, love, and community. Amen

Third Sunday after Epiphany Jonah 3:1-5, 10   Psalm 62:5-12
January 22, 2006   I Cor. 7:29-31   **Mark 1:14-20**

Our gracious, eternal God, we thank you that Jesus' call to his disciples came in such an uneventful way. Contrary to the wisdom of the world he did not start with the privileged and the wealthy and the powerful. He did not begin with those who had little need and little desire for change. He began with some very simple folk. He began with some fishermen.

We pray that his call, "Come, follow me," might again reverberate through our souls today.

- May we hear again the challenge to be your disciples.
- May we hear again the message of this one who brings good news.
- May we hear again the invitation to come to you, "all you who are weary and heavy laden."
- May we hear again eternal words of hope which tell us that however dark the world becomes the darkness cannot ever overcome the radiant light of this holy one, Jesus.
- May we hear again those simple words: "Come, follow me," and may we come, just as we are, and know again the depth of your grace and love for us.

Give us the power to bring change and transformation to the peoples of the world as did those early fishermen. Give us the power to provide the same kind of hope for the world-weary as they brought to theirs. Give us the vision of a world transformed.

We pray for those whose health is a constant and major concern. Be especially with those whose health is compromised so much that they have no hope of ever feeling totally well again. For those we ask that you give courage for the frustrating obstacles of life. Amen

Our gracious God, God of time, God of the seasons, we thank you for the quietness of these mid-winter days with their long evenings. If winter brings to any a bit of dis-ease and depression we ask that you would provide light and hope. May we use these days well. We thank you that they give us the opportunity to ponder the pattern our lives have been weaving and the time to reflect.

- Are our lives going in the direction that is providing us meaning and fulfillment?
  If not, help us to take corrective action and to change.
- Are we using our time in ways that are satisfying?
  If not, help us to take corrective action and to change.
- Are we finding ways to grow in our spiritual journey and to grow more gracious spirits?
  If not, help us to take corrective action and to change.
- Are we growing in our ability to learn tolerance, to be appreciative of the diversity of the peoples you have put on our earth, to overcome our past prejudices?
  If not, help us to take corrective action and to change.
- Are we gaining on some of the more elusive virtues such as humility, generosity, and the ability to provide blessing and affirmation for others?
  If not, help us to take corrective action and to change.
- Are we more embedded within the Christian community, walking hand in hand with our sisters and brothers in the faith?
  If not, help us to take corrective action and to change.
- Are we hopeful people with an attitude to believe that we can overcome the world?
  If not, help us to take corrective action.

O God, help us to use these winter days wisely. Amen

Fifth Sunday after Epiphany   Isaiah 40:21-31   Psalm 147:1-11, 20c
February 5, 2006   I Cor. 9:16-23   **Mark 1:29-39**

O holy One, we come to you in need of your leading and instruction. We so often become bogged down in the details of life and forget to see the bigger picture of life and its needs. We so often give ourselves to what we think is necessary and fail to see what is needful. Forgive us our short-sightedness and save us from our spiritual myopia.

We have been reminded today of how Jesus met needs all about him but did not succumb to the tyranny of demands and many clamouring voices. Help us to follow his example.

- Whereas we tend to think in terms of doing things primarily where we live he thought of people elsewhere who had needs.
- Whereas we tend to take our signals from others he took his direction from within.
- Whereas we tend to live life at a frenetic pace he went out to the desert alone and prayed to find renewal.
- Whereas we tend to be provincial in the scope of our concerns he thought of other communities who needed the good news.

As we walk the Christian journey we pray that you will provide us a greater vision. Interrupt our frenetic activity. Help us to find the creative spiritual pause which will make clearer our mission and refresh us for it. Help us to see all people as your people and to know that we have the responsibility to love them. Help us to have the courage to change the way we have gone about life and to make it both more rewarding and more fruitful.

We ask your care for all of the suffering of the world. Be with those who are living with the effects of natural disasters. Be with those who are living with the effects of war. Be with those who are hungry. Be with those who are homeless. Provide them comfort. Amen

Sixth Sunday after Epiphany   2 Kings 5:1-14   Psalm 30
February 12, 2006   I Cor. 9:24-27   **Mark 1: 40-45**

Eternal God, coming to us in so many ways, and coming to us as a gracious and caring healer, we thank you for beautiful days, for beautiful mountains, and for beautiful trees for us to behold. You have made our world with such lavish beauty there are many times we cannot take it all in because it is so overwhelming.

We thank you also for the healer, Jesus. We thank you that you care about our infirmities and illnesses. We thank you that he was often moved to compassion by the needs of those he encountered. We thank you that he reached out to the most needy of his society and provided them healing and wholeness.

We pray this day for all those who face illness and because of it internal stress and anxiety.

- We pray that you would provide your healing touch for them.
- We pray that you would be with them when they are anxious and fearful and provide them a sense of your quieting and steadying peace.
- We pray that you would give them courage to face difficult decisions and difficult days.
- We pray that you would give them stamina and strength when they seem overwhelmed by weakness.
- We pray that you would give them hope during the dark days.
- We pray that you would be with those cancer survivors who live always grateful but also always on the edge and whose lives are punctuated by periodic checkups which could bring them bad news.

Be with them all and grant them peace.

Be also with our world. Especially be with all of those unstable places marked by violence and hatred. We pray that the world might one day know peace. Amen

<u>Seventh Sunday after Epiphany</u> Isaiah 43:18-25   Psalm 41
February 19, 2006   2 Cor. 1:18-22 **<u>Mark 2: 1-12</u>**

O holy One, we bow in humility before you. We come today a bundle of confusion. We have confusion about our own real needs. We become torn and divided over our values and lose sight of what is of real value. We have confusion about how to approach you and about what to ask. We are so like the paralytic, coming for our physical needs but forgetting our needs of the spirit. Help us this day to see our need of forgiveness.

- Forgive us for our misdirection and missing the mark in our religious journey.
- Forgive us for our difficulty in stretching and reaching for new growth.
- Forgive us for resisting so strongly when change is required of us.
- Forgive us when we shirk from commitment because the cost is too high.
- Forgive us for our insensitivity to the needs of the world about us.
- Forgive us for those times when we fail to listen to the words of others because we do not agree with them.
- Forgive us for shutting out the sufferings of others because of the inner pain which it causes us and because it would involve us in some sacrifice.
- Forgive us for shutting out from our lives any of your children because they are of a different religion or a different skin color or a different sex or a different sexual orientation.
- Forgive us all of our foolish ways.

We pray that you would approach us this day and bring us a wholeness we have not known before. Unite and heal the scattered energies of our spirits so that we may arise from our paralysis of spirit and walk. Amen

Our gracious, eternal God, we come before you with profound gratitude and praise today.

- We thank you that you have sent your voice reverberating through our human history and have never abandoned us to the always prevalent despair in the world.
- We thank you that you continue to knock on our hearts' doors to lift us up, to raise our vision, and to reach for victory in living.
- We thank you for the very gift of life and each day you grant to us.
- We thank you for the hard days which come our way and which cause us to find greater strength, but which in retrospect make the good days all the more appreciated.
- We thank you for the beautiful place in which we live with so many lakes tucked in between the hills and the forests.
- We thank you for our colleagues in the faith from whom we find nurture, strength, and support in times of trouble.
- And we thank you for all those challenges to our spirits which make us bigger people.

Give us the vision of a world and a church yet to be. Enable us to present ourselves a living sacrifice. Enable us to stretch our efforts and reach our goals, hand in hand, because each of us is important in the body of Christ. Give us those moments when, like the disciples, we look around but we see Jesus only. Lead us to the mountaintop but lead us also back to serve your people and to serve your world.

Be with those walking through life's valleys: the bereaved and the broken, the discouraged and the depressed; those recovering from difficult surgeries. Grant them comfort and strength. Amen

O holy one, we bow this day with hope and promise. We thank you for the stories which have empowered people through the ages and given them hope. Make us people who also know your promise.

- May we know the promise you made to Noah that you do not care about destruction and retribution.
- May we know the promise of the rainbow, symbol of hope and symbol of your everlasting covenant with your people.
- May we know the promise of deliverance from sin and renewal of life.
- May we know the promise of your holy One, Jesus, who invites us to become people of the Way and people of discipleship.
- May we know the promise and rewards which a life of discipline brings.
- May we know the promise of eternal life and the hope that whether living or dying you will always hold us close.
- May we know the promise that in our discipleship you will be with us to the ends of the earth.

We ask that you attend us on our Lenten journey. We are so far from being finished products that we need your continued guidance. Help us to focus our spirits on goals that are difficult and as yet unachieved. Teach us how to pray. Teach us humility. Teach us how to relate to others so that they know they are loved and nurtured and received. Teach us to listen well and to understand the other before we respond. Teach us patience. Teach us gentleness toward others and with ourselves. And teach us to receive your gentle grace.

Bless those whose lives are hard and punctuated with illness, grief, and suffering. Amen

Eternal God, we thank you for the longer days of sunlight as we move toward the springtime, for this season of penitence, for these moments of meditation. If we are not already so, cause us to be a grateful and thankful people. Help us to see the blessings each day brings. Help us to see the thoughtful gestures of those around us. Help us to see the beauties of the earth. Help us to see the richness of our Christian heritage. Help us to see the satisfaction in doing something well. Help us to see the workings of your hand in our lives.

Give us also the far-off vision of things yet unseen.

- Like Abraham help us to believe that you create a rich future for us.
- Like Abraham help us to believe that you are still speaking and doing a new thing.
- Like Abraham, who laughed at your promise and failed to take it seriously, may you challenge us to believe in the impossible.
- Like Abraham help us to have the courage to engage in the religious journey and to present our questions and our scepticism but always to find creative conversation with you.
- Like Abraham, who earlier stepped out on faith to journey to a new land, help us to take risks and be willing to venture forth in trepidation but also in faithfulness.
- And like Abraham, help us to be faithful to your everlasting covenant and know you richly as our God.

We pray for our world which always teeters on the edge of turmoil. Give us statesmen for these days who are less interested in being powerful and more interested in being caring and doing right. Give us hope. Amen

We come to you gracious God, ancient of days, awed by your steady unveiling depicted by the biblical story. Episode after episode unveil a greater awareness and a greater understanding of your relationship with your people. We thank you for your ancient covenant which began with Moses. Remind us anew this day that our covenant with you also involves both consequences and commitments on our part.

- Help us to experience enough of your awesome holiness so that we will worship and serve and adore you.
- Help us not to confuse the things or the causes of earth or to value them above you.
- Help us provide you appropriate honour and find room in our lives for worship, solitude, and healing renewal.

May we also find it within ourselves to take seriously your commands which relate to our brothers and sisters.

- Help us to honour not only our parents but all others whom you place in our paths.
- Help us to respect others and to have a firm commitment not to violate them in any way but always to treat them with dignity as your children.
- Help us to work for and maintain integrity and honesty in all of our dealings with others and to refuse to take advantage of others in any way.
- Help us to find satisfaction in the good things in life you have granted to us and not succumb to covetousness, envy, and wanting what others have.

Make new and exciting our journey of the spirit and help us to know that you have sealed your covenant with us by making Jesus not our judge but our friend. Amen

Eternal God, we bow this day on our Lenten journey. We are very aware of our need to retool our souls. Like the ancient people we struggle with the same issues with which they struggled. Like them we are **impatient.**

- We want things to go our way and we want them to do so immediately.
- We don't want to invest the time it takes to provide the nurture and the perspective our spirits need to grow.
- We fail to see the slow and small ways which you provide for our growth.

Help us to trust in you when our way is not clear. Help us to walk by faith. Help us to risk when we are fearful and to temper our impatience.

Like the ancients we are also a very **grumbling and complaining people** living in a negative culture. It is easy to complain, O God. It is easy to be negative. Forgive us for taking the easy road.

- Help us to look upon life as good.
- Help us in hard times to see the glass of life as half full rather than half empty.
- Help us to rejoice as we live and walk in your beautiful world.
- Help us to see the world afresh as a child sees it: with excitement and wonder and joy.
- Help us to see in every challenge not an obstacle but a possibility for achievement.

Refashion and mould our spirits and make us positive people who can make an impact upon our world.

We pray for those troubled places of the earth where violence reigns and where people suffer from wanton attacks. Swing low over all violence and temper the hearts of the hateful. Amen

Fifth Sunday in Lent   **Jeremiah 31:31-34**   Psalm 51:1-12 or 119:9-16
April 2, 2006   Hebrews 5:5-10   John 12:20-33

Our gracious, eternal God, we pause and acknowledge your presence now and always in our lives. We acknowledge our deep needs to learn how much you love us and to learn how to receive your love. We confess that it is easier to think that you are against us when we sin and do wrong. It is easy for us to fall into behaviours which are self-condemning and set up barriers which keep us from being bathed and healed by the power of your love for us. Remind us that you love us so dearly. Remind us that your covenant with us has always been to embrace us rather than to punish us.

- Penetrate our barriers and our false pride whenever we become overcome by self-condemnation.
- Take us by the hand, lead us in your ways.
- Put your law within us and write it on our hearts.
- Help us to know the truth of the words you spoke through Jeremiah that you "will remember our sin no more."

We pray also for our human family. We so often do not have the vision to include everyone in it. We witness so much brokenness and violence.

- We pray for peace in all corners of the earth.
- We pray for less bitterness among groups, factions, tribes, and nations.
- We pray for those whose lives are lived in poverty.
- We pray for those for whom the doors of opportunity are closed.

Remedy the wrongs of this world. Give us the vision of a world in which we demonstrate our covenant with you by also demonstrating your love toward our neighbours. Give us the will to work for the day when all peoples of the earth have food, education, and opportunity to fulfill themselves. Help us to provide healing for the brokenness of all your children. Amen

Liturgy of the Passion   Isaiah 50:4-9a   Psalm 31:9-16
April 9, 2006   Philippians 2:5-11 **Mark 14:1-15:47** or
                                  Mark 15:1-39, (40-47)

___

Our gracious, eternal God, we bow in awe as we acknowledge your powerful presence throughout our human history. As with your people through the ages we ask for your power and influence in our lives.

- Be the source of our strength when we are weak.
- Be the solid rock beneath our feet when we wander or waver.
- Be our shield and wrap your protective arm around us when we are in danger.
- Be the truth that challenges our minds and stretches us to a greater depth of awareness and understanding.
- Be the inspiration of our hearts when life is drab and dreary.
- Be the comfort for our souls when life is harsh.
- Be our guide when we are walking through the valley of decision.

We thank you on this day for your holy one, Jesus. As he set his face toward Jerusalem so help us to set our faces toward our mission and calling. May we listen to his words. May we listen to the better angels of our own selves which he empowers. May we learn to trust more deeply. May we learn to love more fully and be committed to the service of others. May we learn greater mastery in our Christian walk.

Be with those among us with special needs and look upon them with your favour. For those living with the emptiness of grief we ask your loving companionship. Be with those facing changes in their lives because of diminished health. Be with our world which is daily punctuated with strife and conflict and bring greater peace and justice to the earth. Amen

Easter Day   Acts 10:34-43 or *Isaiah 25:6-9*   Ps. 118:1-2, 14-24
April 16, 2006   I Cor 15:1-11 or *Acts 10:34-43*   John 20:1-18 or
Mark 16:1-8

Our gracious, eternal God, we thank you again for another Easter day which reminds us of your victory over death and of our eternal hope. We have many things for which to be thankful as we celebrate the resurrection.

- We thank you for the living one, Jesus, who came to his huddled, fearful band and breathed new life into them.
- We thank you for the fire which was kindled in them for faith.
- We thank you for the hesitant, questioning manner they received the good news.
- We thank you that you make room in your band for the uncertain and the doubters.
- We thank you for the zeal with which they spread the good news.
- We thank you for the continuing reminders that you did not give up on them; and neither do you give up on us.

Teach us, O eternal one and guide us on our journey.

- Teach us the ability to trust.
- Teach us the ability to surrender our cares to you, knowing that you love us with an everlasting love.
- Teach us the ability to live confidently, to accept those times and moments when life is unclear or confused, and to trust that you lead us gently onward.

Resurrect the hopes of our world when its peoples fall into despair over war, continued unrest, conflict, and genocide in so many parts of the world. Swing low and melt the hearts and minds of people that we may change our behaviours. Give us all a greater and brighter vision of how things might be. Bring us peace. Amen

Eternal God, we praise you, the alpha and the omega, the beginning and the end. We praise you for your presence through the long march of our human history. We praise you that you have never left us bereft and without a witness to you when the world seems the darkest to us. Speak to us again this day. Speak to us again your gentle word of peace.

- Grant us your peace when our lives turn difficult and when we seem to be wandering and confused.
- Grant us your peace when we are vulnerable and frightened.
- Grant us your peace when we are walking through uncertain valleys and the next step seems only to hold foreboding for us.
- Grant us your peace when our health is threatened and when we feel fearful that our future may be limited or terminal.
- Grant us your peace when our sense of your presence is thin and like Job we feel as if we are among the forgotten of your people.
- Grant us your peace when our economic security is threatened and when our fears about tomorrow well up and overwhelm us.
- Grant us your peace when our questions and doubts seem stronger than our faith and trust, and give us courage to face them and live them until we come again to a greater certainty.

In all of life may we hear again and again the words of Jesus: "**Peace be with you.**"

We ask your care for all who are carrying heavy burdens. Be with the sick. Be with the grieving. Be with the war-weary. Be with the hungry. Be with the poor. Grant them all your love and compassion. Amen

Third Sunday of Easter   Acts 3:12-19   Psalm 4

April 30, 2006   I John 3:1-7   **Luke 24:36b-48**

Good Shepherd of our souls, we bow with gratitude in our hearts today.

- We thank you for the lavish hospitality with which you have surrounded us.
- We thank you for your gracious love and care for us.
- We thank you for the abundance which you have placed on our plates each day.
- We thank you for the strength which comes from knowing that when life meets us with danger you are our rock and beneath us are your everlasting arms.
- We thank you for the assurance that this is your world and there are many places of goodness and kindness and mercy in it.

Yet we confess that we are so much like those early disciples to whom you said, "Peace be with you." We are often frightened. We are often doubtful. We are often disbelieving. We are often wondering. We are as human and as frail of spirit as were they. Yet we find great comfort in being like them because it gives us hope. You call us as you called them to be your witnesses. As you did not disqualify them for your service neither do you disqualify us.

- Help us to know that their task is our task and that to us also come the words: "You are witnesses of these things."
- Help us to find the joy and excitement of being your witnesses.
- Help us to reach out to our world, so often in despair, and to present the message of forgiveness of sins.
- Help us to be faithful and to be your peacemakers.

O God, grant us the power to fulfill our calling. Amen

O God, whose people have called you by so many different names. Your people have called you Yahweh; they have called you Elohim; they have also called you father. We thank you that somehow the metaphor of "shepherd" also became such a powerful description for you because it evokes feelings of calm, security, and gentleness within us. We thank you that you also sent us Jesus, the Good Shepherd.

- Make us faithful followers of the Good Shepherd.
- When we stray keep us from serious danger and lead us gently back to you.
- Lead us to the places in life where there is enough calm and quiet that we find renewal, but provide us enough challenge to bring out the best in us.
- In those places of life where we become fearful and anxious be with us, keep us safe from danger, and lead us through the valleys of the deep shadows.
- In those times when we face economic uncertainty and worry about tomorrow remind us that "you prepare a table before us."
- Give us the ability to trust your faithfulness to us.
- And in those times when we take a longer look at life and beyond help us to trust that "goodness and mercy shall follow us all the days of our life" and to know that we are yours forever.

We pray for those with special needs. Be with the recently retired who are adjusting to life without a set schedule and who find greater leisure both a joy and a burden because new purposes are yet undefined. Be with those whom we send to war whose lives are filled with great danger, sorrow, and tragedy. Be with the sick and the dying. Be with the needy. Be with those are faced with temptation. Hover over them all and provide comfort and courage. Amen

Fifth Sunday of Easter	**Acts 8:26-40**	Psalm 22:25-31
May 14, 2006	1 John 5:1-6	John 15:1-8

Eternal God, we bow today, each of us with different needs.
- Some of us have experienced triumph; others have known defeats.
- Some have experienced great joy; others have known deep sorrow.
- Some have exulted in good health; others have heard bad news or are facing some physical threat.
- Some have experienced a meaningful acceptance; others have experienced a profound rejection.
- Some have experienced a great gain; others have experienced some losses.
- Some feel confident of the future; others feel only uncertainty and anxiety.

Whatever our needs be today we ask for your power in our lives. There is no need which cannot be faced when we present it to you. So we ask for your power in our weakness. Be also with those for whom life goes smoothly and well. May they pause in gratitude for your gracious blessings when such is the case.

We pray that you would heighten our sense of community and our responsibility for others. Give us the ability to walk with our sisters and brothers and to be open to one another. As Philip got in the carriage and sat with and taught the Ethiopian, may we be willing to bear one another's burdens. May we be willing to set aside our agendas and schedules for another's needs. May we too find a way to bond with those whom you set in our path and to be witnesses to the good news.

We pray that you would bless this needy world. Bring justice and peace. Empower us so that we will not be daunted by the difficulty of working for justice, peace, and equity among all the peoples of the world. Amen

Eternal God, in these moments of quiet we thank you for your presence in our lives. We thank you for all of the testimonies of your profound love for your children. We especially thank you this day for the holy one Jesus. We thank you for his humility. We thank you that rather than elevating himself above us he instead would lift us up and as with his disciples call us "friends." We thank you for his many reminders that we are to love one another. But we confess that we have great difficulty following his command to love.

- We become upset with others and find it easier to reject them than to seek to understand and to love them.
- We struggle with the almost impossible command to love our enemies.
- We become driven to meet our own needs and become blind to the needs of others.
- We are driven to succeed which becomes all consuming and trumps our command to love.

Forgive us our foolish ways. Help us to keep in our awareness this command to love which Jesus repeated so many times. Help us especially to hear it in those hard times when it is most difficult to love.

- Help us to love others when they are power hungry.
- Help us to love others when they are inconsiderate.
- Help us to love others when they are angry and lash out blindly.
- Help us to love others when they are selfish and insensitive.

Help us, O God, to love others so that we may abide in your love and act like the friends of Jesus. Amen

Seventh Sunday of Easter	Acts a:15-17, 21-26	Psalm 1
May 28, 2006	I John 5:9-13	John 17:6-19

Our gracious, eternal God, we thank you for the challenges which life brings. It also brings changes which sometimes throws us into crisis. Be with us in such times in our Christian community. Like the early disciples help us in our common life to find your guidance in our collective decisions.

- Help us to approach our decisions seeking your guidance through prayer.
- Help us to examine our own hearts for any unseemly motives.
- Help us to focus on the common good and not be driven by our own selfish interests.
- Help us to seek consensus and never be satisfied with power plays and divisiveness.
- Help us all to share in our mutual ministry.

Lead us forward and help us to create a community where love, acceptance, and mutuality are expressed, where joy abounds, and where results are achieved because we are all working hand in hand together. May it be said of us as it was said of old: "See how those Christians love one another."

We ask that you would save us from ever being a cloistered cell which seeks escape from our world. Instead, open the windows of our souls to the world and its needs. Send us forth to herald the good news of Jesus, to be your servants to those in need, to visit the sick and the imprisoned, to remember the forgotten in our society, and to work for justice and peace. Use our varied gifts so that as Peter suggested we all might do our fair share in this ministry. Bolster us in moments when we feel inadequate for the task and give us courage. Amen

Day of Pentecost **Acts 2:1-21** or *Ezekiel 37:1-14* Psalm 104:24-34, 35b
June 4, 2006   Romans 8:22-27   John 15:26-27; 16.4b-15
___

O God of power, we bow before you on this Pentecost day and ask that your holy spirit empower us for the daunting task of engaging our world in this time. Like the violent wind that filled the house on that first Pentecost day invade our awareness and fill us with boldness and power.

- Bring a time when we all are willing to listen to and understand others and where communication barriers are overcome.
- Bring a time when the young have a larger vision than just their own selfish dreams.
- Bring a time when the old are not satisfied just to rest and enjoy life but continue to dream dreams of building a better world and commit to achieving it.
- Bring a time when your church is excited and on fire because it knows and serves the God of the Pentecost experience.
- Bring a time when your church engages in alleviating the sufferings and injustices of the world.
- Bring a time when all Christians work together and when partisan bickering is past.
- Bring a time when no group any longer claims it is superior to others and has an exclusive hold on the truth.
- Bring a time when there is tolerance and respect and understanding for the differences of others.
- Bring a time when all Christians stand together in unity and in love.

O God, bring us anew your Pentecost fire and fill us with boldness and power. Amen

| **Trinity Sunday** | **Isaiah 6:1-8** | Psalm 29 |
| June 11, 2006 | Romans 8:12-17 | John 3:1-17 |

O eternal God of the ages, ineffable in mystery, beyond our comprehension, yet placing an insatiable desire for you within the human breast, we bow in awe and humility this day. With your people from all ages we bow, we worship, and we say:

"Holy, holy, holy is the LORD of hosts;
The whole earth is full of (your) glory."

Like Isaiah we know that we are not worthy to approach you. But also like him, we have the tenacity to hold on and insist that we too have seen you.

- We have seen you when as a child we became aware of your mystery.
- We have seen you when we have beheld the wonders of our created world with its splendour and its majesty and color.
- We have seen you when we have seen selfless acts of mercy and compassion performed by one of your caring children.
- We have seen you in those quiet moments when your presence made an indelible impression upon us and we were aware that you have appointed us a destiny to fulfill.
- We have seen you in the courage of those who remind us that there is a moral order which demands justice for all your children.

Renew our covenant with you this day. Blot out our sins and cause our guilt to depart. Help us to live victorious lives because we have been cleansed by your grace and mercy. And fit us to respond to your call as did Isaiah and say: "Here am I, send me." Send us and use us, O God. Amen

Proper 6 (11) I Sam. 15:34-16:13 or *Ezekiel 17:22-24* Psalm 20 or
June 18, 2006   *Psalm 92:1-4, 12-15*   2 Cor. 5:6-10, 14-17 or
                   2 Cor. 5:6-17   **Mark 4:26-34**

Eternal God, we thank you today for this beautiful garden valley in which we dwell. We thank you for the nearby mountains with its forests. We thank you for the magnificent ocean which is close enough for us to enjoy. We are extremely blessed to be sojourners in your beautiful world and we are grateful.

We ask your blessing on this journey of faith to which we have been called. We confess that very often the seen world seems much stronger than the unseen and that the world of certainty and sense seems much stronger than the world of faith and trust and risk. We look at the needs of the world and the daunting task of meeting even a small part of them seems overwhelming and impossible. We need your help, O God. Help us this day to experience the power of faith which Jesus likened to a grain of mustard seed.

- Help us to know that by faith your church can still move mountains.
- Help us to know and to trust that even though we cannot see the results of our efforts immediately that there is something growing and coming to fruition and good will come.
- Help us to know that life is better when we live with expectation and hope rather than pessimism and gloom and disillusionment.
- Help us to know in spite of all of the assaults of evil in our world that you are still working in and through us.
- Help us to scatter the seed of faith and to trust in your quiet working for good.

We need your help, O God. Increase our faith. Amen

Proper 7 (12)   1 Sam. 17(1a, 4-11,19-23), 32-49 or *Job 38:1-11*
June 25, 2006   Psalm 9:9-20 (*optionally with 1 Sam. 17:57-18:5, 10-16) or*
Psalm 107:1-3, 23-32   2 Cor. 6:1-13   **Mark 4:35-41**

Eternal God, we are almost embarrassed to present our prayers to you some days. We realize that when things go well we do not think to pray. We think of you in times of trouble. In our prayers we so often come to you when the storms of life rage and we feel threatened and vulnerable. Many times we carry in our breasts the protest and lament of the Psalmist and wonder how long the storm will persist. We try to have faith but the demons of fear and worry frequently overcome us. In such times when the waves of life roll high speak to us again your gentle word of peace. Bolster us with Jesus' words: "Do not fear, only believe."

- Bring us your peace when we are upset and in turmoil because of the senseless chaos which continually rages in our world.
- Bring us your peace when we feel vulnerable, when our health is threatened, and when we become frightened and worry about how many tomorrows remain for us.
- Bring us your peace when the darker shadow of our inner selves seems too strong and we are overwhelmed and too frightened to acknowledge it and integrate it into our beings.
- Bring us your peace when we are worried about tomorrow and when we worry about whether our money will last as long as we live or how we will make financial ends meet.
- Bring us your peace, O Lord, and quiet our inner storms and help us to trust. Amen

Proper 8 (13)   II Sam. 1:1, 17-27 or *Wisdom of Sol. 1:13-15, 2:23-24*
July 2, 2006   Psalm 130 or *Psalm 30 (optionally with Lamentations 3.23-33)*
       2 Corinthians 8:7-15   Mark 5:21-43

Our gracious, eternal God, as we approach the Independence Day of our great nation we pause to express our profound gratitude for your many blessings to us. We thank you for those who risked their lives and their fortunes to establish this republic in a democratic fashion. We thank you for the vision of a land with freedom and opportunity. We thank you for the values which motivated and drove our founding fathers and mothers to provide for the free expression of religion, yet protected us against the bias of any religion from extending too long an arm of influence over others. We thank you for the checks and balances written into our constitution to protect us all from tyranny by a few. We thank you for the vision and hope of democracy. And we thank you for the continuing vision to work for a more perfect union.

Give us the courage in our time to embrace their values and to find ways to make our nation more temperate and more just. Help us to follow the vision of St. Paul. Help us to excel not only in the virtues of character but to excel in seriously developing generous spirits to aid the needy peoples of the earth. Help us to work for that more excellent way of love.

As we go about the business of being citizens in this great land protect us from succumbing to the shallowness of cheap slogans and simplistic solutions to difficult problems. Protect us from divisiveness and disrespect for those who differ from us. Protect us from cynicism about the future and denying the power of hope because we mistakenly long for a simpler world and think our best days are past. Challenge us to assume our responsibility for the fabric of our life together and to work for justice. Amen

Our gracious God, we bow in gratitude and express our praise
to you this day. You have planted us in a most beautiful part of the
world. We praise and thank you for your goodness.

- We thank you for the beauty of our lakes surrounded by
  magnificent pines which reach to the sky.
- We thank you for the hills and valleys and for winding
  country roads which bring us to behold beauty we did not
  know existed.
- We thank you for those serendipitous moments when
  we come across wildlife and when your world of nature
  becomes alive and vibrant and exciting.
- We thank you for the sounds of the woods.
- We thank you for the different and beautiful songs of the
  birds and for the splendid beauty with which you have
  painted them differently and with such striking colors.
- We thank you for the serenity of sunset skies ablaze with
  pinks, oranges, and purples.
- We thank you for many moments of solitude when we feel
  the peace and harmony.

In these summer months renew us for the Christian journey.
Instruct us for ministry in our time. Send us forth with authority as
you sent your disciples.

- Teach us how to be sensitive to the culture in which we
  live and to hear and understand its needs.
- Teach us how to frame the good news for our time.
- Teach us how to trust you in the journey of life and to
  know that you go before us.
- Teach us how to gain mastery over the demons of modern
  life and to live abundant lives. Amen

Eternal God, utterly beyond us, we thank you that you are also within us else we would not have the presumption to address you. When we hear the Psalm about your creativity we are reminded of your awesomeness. We want to join with the ancient and sing the ancient song:

"The earth is the LORD'S and all that is in it,

The world, and those who live in it...."

We pray that we too might ask the Psalmist's question and do some self-examination on our spiritual journey, when he said: "Who shall ascend the hill of the LORD?"

- Are we deepening our commitment to you?
  HELP US TO ANSWER TRUTHFULLY.
- Are we demonstrating love and consideration for all the people we meet daily?
  HELP US TO ANSWER TRUTHFULLY.
- Are we being honest and truthful in our relationships or do we bevel the edges of our integrity in order to gain an advantage over others?
  HELP US TO ANSWER TRUTHFULLY.
- Are we growing in our ability to include all people in the scope of our concern?
  HELP US TO ANSWER TRUTHFULLY.
- Are we working to achieve justice for all or do we care most about our own gain?
  HELP US TO ANSWER TRUTHFULLY.
- Are we putting our energies on the side of peace rather than war?
  HELP US TO ANSWER TRUTHFULLY

Having answered help us as we bow gratefully to step boldly into your holy place and receive your grace, and to go forth renewed for life's journey. Amen

Proper 11 (16) 2 Samuel 7:1-14a or *Jeremiah 23:1-6* Psalm 89:20-37 or
July 23, 2006 *Psalm 23* Ephesians 2:11-22 **Mark 6:30-34, 53-56**

Our gracious God, we pause these moments for a time of rest and renewal. The world is so much with us and we frequently lose our sense of perspective. Sometimes we engage in frenetic activity simply to avoid looking inward. Other times we simply are stressed by all of the commitments in which we are engaged. Help us to follow Jesus' example and find a quiet place and rest awhile.

- Help us to assess the direction our lives are going and to change our course if necessary.
- Help us to find time to nurture the interior journey of our spirits and to make moments when we can be in touch with the eternal.
- Help us with the Psalmist to know that the number of our days is finite and we are only on a journey.
- Help us not to fear the quiet and silence but instead to see it as a time for centering our lives once again.
- Help us, when we have found a quiet place and rested awhile, then to go forward again to reach out in service to this world of people and its needs.

O God, we often feel that the needs of the world are so overwhelming. Help us not to diminish what we might do because of our lack of expectation. Enhance both our vision and our will. Help us to reach out to alleviate the world's suffering. Help us to put our influence on the side of justice and peace. Help us to use our voice to make known our wishes in the political arena where decisions are made which affect people. Help us to give and to share generously where tragedy strikes. Help us to be open to the hurts of others whom you put in our path each week. In all these ways help us to have compassion for your needy children.

Be also with all who need your special graces this day. Amen

Proper 12 (17)   2 Samuel 11:1-15 or *2 Kings 4:42-44*   Psalm 145:10-18 or
July 30, 2006   *Psalm 14*   Ephesians 3:14-21   **John 6:1-21**

Eternal God, we pray that you would help us center ourselves as we pray. Take our minds from all that would distract us. Take from us our fears. Take from us our apprehension about our tomorrows. Take from us our resentments and our angers. Take from us all that is negative and destructive. Instead may we be bathed by your love which will not let us go.

We offer you our gratitude for your many mercies bestowed upon us so generously. You lend us life and you lend us each day, many of which we take for granted. Help us to affirm and use and appreciate each day as your gift to us. You provide so graciously for us. We thank you that we live in a land which has been so blessed with abundance. We have the opportunity for a quality of life and an abundance of goods which is unequalled in human history. Help us to count our blessings and always to give you thanks.

When Jesus bid his disciples to feed the people gathered around him he had compassion upon them. When he came to his friends in the storm he calmed their fears. We thank you that you care about food and fear, two of humankind's enduring concerns. Feed us and calm our fears as we journey from day to day. Give us trust that you walk with us.

Give us the will to share our gifts in order to impact our world and to make it a better place. Use this church and expand the ministry of each of us. When we would be tempted to falter give us courage and a greater vision. Give us the courage to be your faithful people.

We pray for our world and all its people and leaders. May each nation include in its self-interest the least of our sisters and brothers and may each aspire to peace and good will. May the world's leaders aspire to peace. Amen

Proper 13 (18)   2 Samuel 11:26-12:13a or *Exodus 16:2-4, 9-15*
August 6, 2006   Psalm 51:1-12 or *Psalm 78:23-29* **Ephesians 4:1-16**
John 6:24-35

Eternal God, we are of all people extremely blessed. We are blessed because you have rescued us from despair and made us people of hope.

- You have numbered us with the saints of Ephesus and all other cities where your people have gathered and you have made us your own.
- You have claimed us to receive your grace, mercy and peace.
- You have destined us to see the world in a new way and to go forth into it with courage and confidence.
- You have forgiven us our sins, wiped the slate clean, and given us a new resolve and a new joy.
- You have given us an inheritance in an enduring and everlasting hope which you will fulfill for us in the fullness of time.

We thank you, O God, for such a rich inheritance. Help us on our journey to be renewed as we move along the road of life. May we not succumb to the temptations of cynicism or defeat. May we not limit our expectations for life because they are difficult. Instead, may we see problems as possibilities for new growth and achievement. May we stare difficulty in the face and approach it with hope and optimism. Fortify our wills. Call forth our best thinking and creativity. And use us in your enterprise of changing and redeeming the people of your world.

We ask your care for all who are suffering in any way. Be with those who are living in dangerous places and who know the anxiety and destructiveness of war. Be with those in harms way. Be with the innocent people who are in the wrong place at the wrong time. Provide comfort and safety for the living and hope for the dying. Help us to build a world where the causes of war are eliminated. Cure our warring madness, O God, and grant us peace. Amen

Proper 14 (19)   2 Samuel 18:5-9, 15, 31-33 or *1 Kings 19:4-8*
August 13, 2006   Psalm 130 or *Psalm 34:1-8* **Ephesians 4:25-5:2**
              John 6:35, 41-51

O Eternal One, whose message to us has always been that our relationship to you is inextricably related to how we treat our sisters and brothers, bend low your spirit this day and touch us with your power.

- Wean us from our tendency to nurture perceived slights and to put hot coals to our anger.
- Wean us from all tendencies to take advantage of others for personal gain.
- Wean us from negativity and from becoming bitter whether or not we think we are justified in our feelings.
- Wean us from the all too human and common tendency to gossip about others and to slander them in any way.
- Wean us from carrying malice in our hearts and from giving in to anything that would poison relationships with others.

MAKE US OVER AGAIN, O GRACIOUS GOD.

Give us a consistent kindness and compassion for others. Keep us always tender hearted even when the world delivers difficult blows and setbacks to us. Teach us once again about your redeeming grace in order that we may learn, however slowly and however tentatively, how to forgive others. Teach us how to live abundantly into the future as victorious and expectant people, greeting each new day with eagerness and excitement. And indelibly remind us that we are among your forgiven and beloved community.

We present to you all who have special need of your grace today. Keep them in your gracious care and insofar as we are able use us to make their burdens lighter. Be with those who war and who are victims of war and grant to us a peaceful world. Amen

Proper 15 (20)   **1 Kings 2:10-12; 3:3-14** or *Proverbs 9:1-6*

August 20, 2006   Psalm 111 or *Psalm 34:9-14* Ephesians 5:15-20
                              John 6:51-58

Eternal God, we thank you today for your goodness. You have given us beautiful days. You bless us richly with goodness daily. We thank you and praise you.

We live in a time of considerable confusion. We ask today for your wisdom as Solomon asked for wisdom. We are often fearful as was Solomon. We live in a time of peril, war, and world unrest. Different and competing interests strive for our attention and loyalty. Help us, O God, to pray for wise and discerning spirits.

- Give us wisdom to know good from evil.
- Give us wisdom to assess the clamouring voices and concerns with which we are daily bombarded.
- Give us wisdom so that we might learn to be accepting of all the diverse people you have created.
- Give us wisdom to be peacemakers and mediators of understanding where there is conflict.
- Give us wisdom when we are in conflict to make it possible both for us and for those with whom we differ to save face and win and move forward hand in hand.
- Give us wisdom not to violate any of your creatures by discriminating against them.
- Give us wisdom to discern what is of ultimate value for our souls and to make wise choices.

O GOD, GIVE US WISDOM.
O GOD, GIVE US DISCERNMENT.
O GOD, GIVE US THE WILL TO BE FAITHFUL.
O GOD, GIVE US THE POWER TO LOVE. Amen

Proper 16 (21)   **1 Kings 8: (1,6,10-11), 22-30, 41-43** or *Joshua 24:1-2a, 14-18*
August 27, 2006   Psalm 84 or *Psalm 34:15-22*   Ephesians 6:10-20
John 6:56-69

O holy one of Israel and God of our Lord Jesus Christ, we come to you this day standing in a long line of people who have been in awe of your mystery. We have developed our holy places where we might encounter you. Yet your being and presence cannot be captured or contained by our holy dwellings for even the heavens cannot contain you. With Solomon we ask that you would heed our prayers this day.

- Hear the pleas of your servants when we are in need of strength and life is hard.
- Hear the pleas of your servants when we miss the mark and need forgiveness.
- Hear the pleas of your servants when we become lost in our selfish pursuits and fail to have compassion for our neighbours.
- Hear the pleas of your servants when we lose perspective and become prideful and puffed up and are insistent on our own way.
- Hear the pleas of your servants when the influence of the world's events creates in us despair and defeatism.
- Hear the pleas of your servants when we forget that we can change and influence this world.
- Hear the pleas of your servants when we would forget that your grace is for every human being.

HEAR THE PLEAS OF YOUR SERVANTS AND GIVE US VICTORY OVER EVIL.

Help us also to integrate the ideal of Solomon's time always to provide hospitality and welcome to the foreigner because you include all people in our human family. Amen

94

Proper 17 (22)   Song of Solomon 2:8-13 or *Deuteronomy 4:1-2, 6-9*
September 3, 2006   Psalm 45:1-2, 6-9 or *Psalm 15*   ___James 1:17-27___
Mark 7:1-8, 14-15, 21-23

O God, we praise you this day for your graciousness to us. You have not left us bereft and without a road map for life but have provided us with signposts for our religious journey. Continue to be our guide on our way. Lead us to a Christian life which is characterized by authenticity.

- Lead us in those times when there is a disconnect in our lives between what we profess and how we live, those times when we are hearers of the word but not doers.
- Lead us in those times when we are quick to cut people off and refuse to hear them.
- Lead us in those times when we have not carefully weighed what to say but jump to quick and erroneous conclusions and blurt out a hasty and unkind response.
- Lead us in those times when we are quick to anger and unaware of the hurt which often lies behind our anger, thus making difficult the possibility of reconciliation.
- Lead us in those times when the walk we walk does not correlate with the talk we talk.

HELP US TO BE DOERS OF THE WORD AND NOT HEARERS ONLY. Help us to hear the cries of the needy. Help us to be peacemakers in a world which is so characterized by and so familiar with war. Help us to be hopeful people wherever we find despair. Help us never to flag in zeal or become weary in well-doing. Help us to take seriously our mission to the sick, the dying, the disadvantaged, and all those places of the earth where you still call to us through the cries of your children. HELP US TO BE FAITHFUL, O GOD. Amen

Proper 18 (23)   Proverbs 22:1-2, 80-9, 22-23 or *Isaiah 35:4-7a*
September 10, 2006   Psalm 125 or *Psalm 146*   James 2:1-10, (11-13), 14-17
Mark 7:24-37

Eternal God, we come before you this day with a strong presumption. We presume that like the Syrophoenician woman, an outcast with no societal standing, we too are worthy of your time and ear. We thank you that we need not be of any particular nation, race, or gender, for you will listen simply because we are all created and loved by you. At birth you claim all of your children and we are yours.

We thank you for the diversity of all the peoples of the earth even if we fail to understand them. We thank you that Jesus was attentive to those who were diverse and different than he. We thank you that he responded to this woman to whom he at first felt no obligation or commitment. We thank you that he was able to change his mind about her. As he opened his heart to the unbridled demand of those about him so open your hearts to us.

- Cause us to be open to those who differ from us.
- Cause us to have the courage to receive the least of your children.
- Cause us to grow and heal the blindness which would constrict our greater freedom in Christ.
- Cause us to find healing from our past prejudices.
- Cause us to have a welcoming demeanor to all of your children who cross our paths.

Like the woman who was so insistent on behalf of her daughter, meet our deepest needs today. Give us courage to be as insistent as was this woman in seeking your attention. Give to us the ability and trust to know that we are worthy of your attention and healing. Give us the firm conviction that your power, healing, and grace are for all people. Give us fulfillment on our journey. Amen

Proper 19 (24)
September 17, 2006

Proverbs 1:20-33 or *Isaiah 50:4-9a*
Psalm 19 (*optionally with Wisdom of Solomon* 7:26-8:1)or
Psalm 116:1-9   James 3:1-12
Mark 8:27-38

Eternal God, we bow today with a mixture of emotions. We have heard a lesson today which involves both a confession and hard command to deny oneself. We are numbered with all those through the ages who have responded to Jesus' question about who he was. We become uncomfortable as we struggle for our answers.

- We become uncomfortable because the answer is more about us than you.
- We become uncomfortable because we so often struggle for neat, tidy answers and try to pin things down in our understanding.
- We become uncomfortable because we struggle with the implications of truth in a world where there is so much falsehood and spin.
- We become uncomfortable because we know our answer involves us in a driving and lifelong commitment.

O God, lead us to confession and commitment and be with us in our struggles. Help us to make some progress with the hard notion of denying ourselves and losing ourselves in bearing the cross of Jesus. Give to us a real sense of how great the cause of Jesus is. We are in an uphill battle because our culture bombards us with contrary messages. We often succumb to seductive appeals for self improvement with emphasis on "self." We often succumb to the indulgent appeal to consumption. We struggle with our self worth. O God, give us courage and help us to know that we find ourselves when we are found by your grace and give ourselves to a quest which is eternal. Give us the courage and the will to give ourselves to others and to your service. Lead us to confession and to commitment. Amen

Proper 20 (25)   Proverbs 31:10-31 or *Wis. Of Solomon 1:16-2:1, 12-22*
September 24, 2006   Psalm 1 or *Jeremiah 11:18-20 or Psalm 54*
                      James 3:13-4:3, 7-8a   **Mark 9:30-37**

Our gracious eternal God, we praise you today for gracing our lives with consistently sunny, warm, and beautiful days. You have caused us to dwell in a beautiful place with mountains which are breathtaking. We thank you. Though we are followers of Jesus we are a long way from being remade and we struggle with self and ego issues. Like the disciples we bring our insecurity. Like the disciples we want to be the best and the greatest. Like the disciples we claw for power and influence.

- We love to be recognized and to be accorded places of honour.
- We love to be recognized as leaders and to receive praise for what we do.
- We love to be considered the greatest.
- We love to have power and influence while at the same time hating power games and struggles.
- We love, in the power games of life, to win and to come out on top.

We pray that you would save us from our destructive and selfish selves. Give us a vision of service to the community and the world. Give us a cooperative spirit so that the gifts of all may be utilized for good. Transform our power hungry egos into servant egos where we strive only to work your will. Change our jealous natures into generous ones where we seek to work hand in hand with colleagues in the faith and where we seek to build others up. Help us to build community and not worry about who gets credit. Help us to develop humility of heart. Amen

Proper 21 (26)   **Esther 7:1-6, 9-10; 9:20-22** or *Numbers 11:4-6, 10-16, 24-29*
October 1, 2006   Psalm 124 or *Psalm 19:7-14*   James 5:13-20
Mark 9:38-50

Eternal God, we are ever so aware of our ties to the biblical world as we have today entered the world of Esther. We regret that so little has changed in our public life since then.

- There is still intrigue in high places.
- There are still unholy alliances.
- There is still the dynamic of the fearful trying to do away with, or at least to get out of the way, perceived enemies or threats to their power.
- There is still the problem of evil in the guise of good.
- There is still deceit used to gain selfish ends.

So it will be world without end. Yet we ask your aid as we go about building our lives, our nation, and our world in this twenty first century.

- May we not be disillusioned because of the deceit of peoples' hearts.
- May we not lose faith in people because of the faithlessness of the few.
- May we not fail to see this as your wonderful world or be dispirited.
- May we not lose a faithful and expectant spirit which is expectant for good, expectant for hope, expectant for triumph.
- May we not lose hope in the ultimate triumph of good over evil.

As in Esther's day may we not forget to make days of feasting and thanksgiving and gladness and give you thanks for your goodness to us. Be with us, O God, who turns sorrow into gladness, weakness into strength, defeat into triumph. Give us triumphant spirits. Amen

99

Proper 22 (27) **Job 12:1; 2:1-10** or *Genesis 2:18-24* Psalm 26 or 8
October 8, 2006 Hebrews 1:1-4; 2:5-12 Mark 10:2 16

Eternal God, we open our collective souls to your presence. We come needing to empty ourselves of the baggage and cares of the week and in some cases of life. May we come with the trust of a child.

- Some have had heavy burdens to bear and like Job's wife wonder about the fairness of life.
- Some have seen a glimpse of our fragility and mortality and faced the terror and prospect of losing a dear one and come away grateful the dear one has been spared.
- Some have suffered a disappointment.
- Some have been walking through the dark valleys and nights of the soul and have been despondent.
- Some are facing life-changing decisions.

Lord, empty us of our common cares.

- Free us from the demand to hold you to a justice regarding the inequities of life as they apply to us.
- Free us from complaining about life's unfairness.
- Free us from the desire and temptation to clutch and hold close our human treasures.

Teach us the wisdom that it is only in losing ourselves in causes and service which transcend ourselves that we truly find ourselves. Enable us to cast all our cares upon you. Enable us to heed again Jesus' words not to let our hearts be troubled. And fill us with your peace that passes all understanding.

Make us valiant in the service of our world. May we never be discouraged by the difficulty of our Christian vision even though we will never achieve it completely. Grant us courage and perseverance. Amen

Proper 23 (28)   **Job 23:1-9, 16-17** or *Amos 5:6-7, 10-15*
October 15, 2006   Psalm 22:1-15 or *Psalm 90:12-17*
               Hebrews 4:12-16   Mark 10:17-31

Eternal God, we bow this day aware of all of the mysteries of life which will always be beyond our understanding and comprehension. We all either have or will stand in the company of Job and utter our complaints.

- When days go bad we feel as abandoned as did Job and we ask "why?"
- When life is unfair and we feel you are being heavy-handed with our destiny we also complain bitterly.
- When there are no answers we too wonder how you could feel so far away from us and we too wish to know where we might find you.
- When we feel faint of heart and beaten down we too sink into depression and despair.

O God, be near in such times even when we cannot feel you are near. Give us strength and courage and fortitude in the middle of life's most difficult moments.

- Give us the courage to bring our anger and our frustration before you.
- Give us courage to raise our fists in anger and keep conversation with you in our turmoil.
- Give us courage to be open and transparent and honest in our search for you.
- Give us courage to face our fears head on and not wish to hide or deny them.

O GOD, GIVE US COURAGE. GIVE US COURAGE FOR ALL OF LIFE'S STORMS. Through whatever storms life presents we pray that you will give us the ability to trust though we cannot see the way ahead, to maintain hope though life momentarily would drag us to despair, to believe that you will provide us with victory and triumph. Be our God and our guide. Amen

O holy One, we bow today ever aware of our deep thirst for understanding of your ways. We are often like Job and present our questions about life and the universe as if there is going to be some clear answer to the deepest and most difficult issues we face. We want to have answers to the problems of good and evil. We look upon natural disasters and question why they happen. We struggle to rid life of its ambiguity. We struggle to comprehend. We ask that you would be with us in our turmoil. Cause us in life's storms to pause and with the Psalmist to be still and know you. Cause us to live more easily with the ambiguities of life and to realize that many of life's happenings do not yield to an easy understanding. Cause us to bow in awe when we experience the unbridled power of nature. Cause us to bow in awe before you who laid out the heavens and the earth.

We pray also for our world. We have not learned the futility of war as a way to resolve human differences. We project the worst of motives onto our enemies and claim the best for our own. We continue to demonize our enemies in order to justify killing them. We speak of others as evil but deny the evil which resides in us.

Deliver us , O God. Save us from refusing to learn. Help us to revise our lives and our culture so that we may gain a heart of wisdom and know you who are the beginning of wisdom. Bring us greater hope in the future, greater belief in the human family, and less distrust of others. Bring us a better world where love and peace break forth like the springtime.

We commend to you all who suffer from illness, all who have experienced grief and loss, all who are facing unwanted transitions in their lives. Be to them a comforting hope. Amen

Job 42:1-6, 10-17 or *Jeremiah 31:7-9*
Psalm 126 or *Psalm 34:1-8, (19-22)*
Hebrews 7:23-28   **Mark 10:46-52**

Our gracious, eternal God, we give thanks and praise for this new day and for the profound gift of life. Help us as we journey to come to terms with our spiritual blindness. We are so prone to see but not to see, to move so quickly through our minutes, hours and days that we fail to see so much which is important. We are reminded today of our spiritual blindness and how you healed many. May we hear again that powerful word of Jesus, "ephphatha," "be opened." Touch our eyes and hearts that we may be given new and perceptive sight.

- Open our eyes to the magnificent beauty of your created world which we so often miss in our preoccupation with other worries.
- Open our eyes to the needs and hurts of others and give us the sensitivity and compassion to love them through it.
- Open our eyes and hearts to those who go through life discriminated against and help us when they enter our lives to give them a warm and gracious reception.
- Open our eyes to those systems of our society which impede liberty and justice.
- Open our eyes to the deep recesses of evil within the human breast which creates conflict and war.
- Open our eyes to poverty and help us to work for the day when none of your children are denied a place at the table of life.

O GRACIOUS GOD, OPEN OUR EYES.

Keep in your care the suffering and the sick, the dying and the depressed, and all who need your care this day. Amen

Proper 26 (31)   **Ruth 1:1-18** *or Deuteronomy 6:1-9*
Nov 5, 2006   Psalm 146 *or Psalm 119.1-8*
                                     Hebrews 9:11-14   Mark 12:28-34

Our gracious eternal God, we thank you for those in our biblical heritage who have been true and loyal in their commitments. We thank you for a book such as Ruth which was written in a male dominated culture where women had few rights and where they were disenfranchised without their husbands. We thank you for this early heroine in the faith who knew about commitment, love, loyalty, and faithfulness. We pray that we will be enabled to value such commitments in our time.

- Help us to see how love transcends all human differences and national origins.
- Help us to develop integrity and loyalty and have the will to live by what we believe and to sacrifice for others.
- Help us to be faithful to the family and friends with whom we walk and live daily.
- Help us to meet the needs of others even if it comes as a sacrifice for us.
- Help us to make a commitment to love those to whom we are bound as in-laws and to own them as our own as did Ruth.

We ask your care for our world which is so divided. We pray that you would tend those places where people are suffering, where people are wantonly killing people of their own country, where people are fighting for power, where politicians fail to be statesmen and work for special interests rather than the good of all. O God, whose heart must suffer by human cruelty and sin, bring to us the vision of a better world and the will to make it happen. Lead us to a world of love, good will, and peace. Give us the will to work for a better world for all nations and all people. Amen

Our gracious, eternal God, we bow on this stewardship Sunday with feelings of ambivalence and inadequacy. We are often confused in our thinking and in our attitudes about money. For many of us, and for most of our lives, there has never been enough money. So it blows our minds to hear the story of Jesus as he pointed out a poor widow contributing all the money she had to live on. We cannot imagine ourselves taking the kind of risk that woman took. We cannot imagine having the kind of trust she had as she gave all she possessed. We cannot imagine others giving all they have, and we would be critical of their lack of prudence if they did. Most of all, we cannot imagine giving all we have without filling our lives with worry.

O God, nothing like money makes us feel so inadequate and confused. Nothing like money focuses what we treasure. Help us this day with your healing.

- Help us to reorder our priorities in life so that we prize and value what lasts.
- Help us to have a vision of a world made new and a church making an impact for the healing of lives throughout the earth.
- Help us to invest less in the frivolous and more in the enduring.
- Help us to be cheerful givers and not give only out of obligation.
- Help us to give and to expect great things.

On this great day we ask for great things for our church and its ministry. Use our resources. Use our talents and gifts and multiply them all for good. Direct us into those ministries which will provide benefit and blessing for those in need and those hungry for the gospel. Amen

Proper 28 (33)   1 Samuel 1:4-20 or *Daniel 12:1-3*
Nov 19, 2006   I Samuel 2:1-10 or *Psalm 16*
                              Hebrews 10:11-14, *(15-18)*, 19-25
                              Mark 13:1-8

Eternal God, we know that as we bow and pray there are some days when our faces are filled with worry. Sometimes our lives are full of stress and trouble. And always they are filled with wondering what tomorrow might bring. We thank you that we are in the good company of the disciples who were also filled with concerns and wondered about tomorrow. They wished for signs that tomorrow would be alright. They wanted to know what would happen and when. We have not outgrown that need. Tomorrow brings anxiety for all of us.

- We ask in times when we are fearful that you would help us to be more trusting.
- We ask in times of crisis that you would help us to be courageous and resilient and know that you will see us through.
- We ask in times of setbacks that you would give us a renewed vision of what is possible if we put our creativity to full use.
- We ask in times of discouragement or depression that you will give us the hope necessary to go forward.
- We ask in times of inner disequilibrium that you will give us enough power to be victorious over any uncertainty or inner quivering.

O God, in whose time are all times and all endings, be our assurance and bring us your peace.

- In the bleakness known to every generation may we be undaunted in expressing the power and hope of the gospel for our time.
- In the bleakness known to every generation may we not long for signs and a certainty which will always elude us.
- In the bleakness known to every generation may we not expend our energy in anxiousness.

Give to us the ability to trust you into the ages of all ages. Amen

Reign of Christ   2 Samuel 23:1-7 or *Daniel 7:9-10, 13-14*
Nov. 26, 2006   Psalm 132:1-12, (13-18) or *Psalm 93*
                                 Revelation 1:4b-8   John 18:33-37

Our gracious, eternal God, on this last Sunday of the church year we are made more deeply aware of the fleetingness of time and of life. Life is precious and we are also aware that it is precarious.

We thank you that you have enriched our lives by the support of loving family members. During this transition day, and during advent which is coming, life for many among us will still be punctuated by an episodic grief which will come in unexpected and sometimes unwanted times. They will often be reminded of the absence of a loved one. So we ask for strength, comfort, and courage for them. Help us to be sensitive to the grieving and to stand with them in these days.

May we also make these celebration days.

- May we celebrate the victories our loved ones achieved.
- May we celebrate the love they passed on to us and to so many others.
- May we celebrate the faith and belief they lived and which they placed in us.
- May we celebrate the hopes which they dreamed and then went on to achieve.
- May we celebrate the contributions they made to the church and to society.
- May we celebrate their individual uniqueness, a creature of your making, never to be duplicated in all of time.

As we have gathered to celebrate and to remember their lives today may we all trust in you, the "Alpha and the Omega," and may we trust that you give us and our dear ones safe harbour into the ages of all ages. "Blessing and honor, glory and power, be to you"[1] forever and ever.   Amen

---

[1] This phrase is from the Statement of Faith of the United Church of Christ.

<u>Year C</u>

<u>First Sunday in Advent</u>   <u>Jeremiah 33:14-16</u> Psalm 25:1-10
December 3, 2006   I Thess. 3:9-13   Luke 21:25-36

O Eternal God, breaking into our world at unexpected times and in unexpected places, look with favour upon us as we seek once again to prepare the way of the Lord. Visit the desert places of our lives and cause them to rejoice and blossom. O Light of the world, in those times when we have weak spirits and fearful hearts, help us again to hear the echoes from Isaiah's long-ago century to be strong and not to fear. And help us again to find hope in the promise seen by Jeremiah. Impress us once again this year with your presence in our history.

- Impress us with the majesty of your greatness but also with the lowliness of Jesus.
- Impress us with the grand announcement to Mary but also with the simple stirrings of your presence within our lives.
- Impress us with the fear and awesomeness of your presence to the Shepherds but also with the gentle peace which passes all understanding and the words of the angel to "fear not."
- Impress us with the costly gifts of the wise men but also with those human kindnesses which are extended from one to another out of love and thoughtfulness.

We ask again for peace in our world. Temper the hatreds of the earth. Help us to build a world where the reasons for conflict are diminished. Change the hearts of those whose only mission is to maim others. Be with our enemies that we might one day be friends. Be with those in peril and those who suffer. Be with those who must soldier and are far from home. Give to all the world the hope and vision to create a new beloved community. Cradle your world once again and bring us hope. Amen

Eternal God, we come to you during this season of hope. May the power of Jesus be born in us again. Give us the hope expressed in Zechariah's song: "By the tender mercy of our God the dawn from high will break upon us, to give light to those who sit in darkness...."

- Rekindle that hope in those who have grown weary and for whom life is dark.
- Restore hope to those whose present or past lives have become a burden.
- Restore to all of us the vision and excitement of lives which are motivated and lived with a sense of mission and purpose.

If any is imprisoned in a past which is crippling or tenaciously diminishing the possibilities of making life meaningful today provide a way of reframing that past.

- Help them reframe that past so that it no longer imprisons and limits today.
- Help them reframe that past so that it can be transcended.
- Help them reframe that past so that it can be integrated and seen as an asset rich with the ability to understand the human experience and relate to the sufferings of others.

You came, gentle Jesus, to a world of broken people. Come again to us and transform us as you did those who first experienced your touch and grace. Fulfill the hope seen in John the Baptist that your mercy might break forth upon us.

We pray for our world: confused, in constant strife, filled with passion and rage and uncertainty. Hold this world in your compassionate embrace. Help us as a global people to love and care for one another. Amen

Third Sunday of Advent   Zephaniah 3:14-20   Isaiah 12:2-6
Dec. 17, 2006   **Philippians 4:4-7**   Luke 3:7-18

Our gracious, eternal God, we come before you today with gratitude. Grant that we may also find within us the spirit of rejoicing. Help us with Paul to "...rejoice in the Lord always."

- Give to us an attitude which looks on life and says that it is good.
- Give to us an attitude which is hopeful.
- Give to us an attitude which is able to look upon the difficulties and worries of life and to be undaunted by them.
- Give to us an attitude and will to live life in the present moment and not worry about those moments which are coming and which may or may not hold foreboding.
- Give to us an attitude which is insistent on finding the good in life and rejoicing over it.
- Give to us an attitude which Paul suggests so that we may pray with thanksgiving as we make our requests to you.
- Give to us an attitude which is able to possess your peace which passes all understanding.

Walk with us through this advent season, transforming the thinking of our minds so that we might reflect the joy in the good news of the gospel. You have made us new people. In our behaviours may we demonstrate hope and triumph. Release us from all negativity and defeatism and give us victory over all the principalities and power of earth.

We ask your care for our fragile world, O Prince of Peace. Grant to all peoples the vision of a world made new. Grant us the will to work for peace and to find alternative ways of resolving national and international conflict. Grant to all people the will to refuse to take up arms and go to war. Lead us in the ways of peace, O Prince of Peace. Amen

O holy One, we thank you that as we hear the ancient story of your mysterious workings in Jesus from different places in Scripture we hear the same echoes of your mercy and grace. We are reminded that it is you who look with favour upon us as you did with Mary. It is you who have come to us and embraced us with your everlasting love. We do not need to find you for we have already been found by your love.

Be with those for whom this particular Christmas will be difficult.

- Be with those who have known the bitterness of grief.
- Be with those who know hardship or want.
- Be with those whose lives have become unstable or uncertain.
- Be with those whose health is compromised.
- Be with those whose business or jobs are in jeopardy.

Remind us as we go through dark valleys that we go not alone.

- Remind us that the light of the world cannot be extinguished by the darkness.
- Remind us that even in darkness there is the possibility of hope within the human breast.
- Remind us that you cradle us with your love as once you cradled the world in Jesus.
- Remind us that you wish us to be victorious people who overcome the world.

Be with those whose hope is diminished today. Be with the homeless, the weary, the over-worked, the hungry, the refugees, the suffering children of the world, and hold them close to you. May a better world be born: a world with love, justice, and peace. Amen

Eternal God, as we come to a new year and ponder the meaning of time, we pray that you would be with us as we are about the sober task of numbering our days. As we do so may we gain a heart of wisdom. As we reflect upon all of the endless possibilities of creation we are overwhelmed that you gently called each one of us into being. That we were a thought to you before our birth, that you gave us a name, that you made us all in our own uniqueness when you could have fashioned someone else, to us this is a mystery. We thank you for your creative love which made us and for your redeeming love which makes us whole. We thank you for those moments in our developmental lives when our parents brought us faithfully to be in the worshipping community even as Jesus was brought to and was found in the Temple. Hear our requests today.

- Help us to receive each new day as a gift and not as a burden.
- Help us to see every day as an opportunity to be seized.
- Give us courage when we would find it easier to cower.
- Give us mountains to climb when we would rather dwell in the valleys.
- Forbid that the difficulty of living well and doing your will should ever foster in us despair.
- Instead give us power even in our weakness to overcome.

We bring before you all of the special needs in our community: those recovering from illness or affliction; those recovering from surgery; those whose lives know the shadow of death; those who mentally are gradually leaving their loved ones due to Alzheimer's disease; those who know the darkness of depression. Touch each with your grace. Touch our war-weary world and be especially with those who have been devastated by the consequences of war. Bring peace and recovery to the nations and a will to live in harmony. Amen

Epiphany of the Lord   Isaiah 60:1-6   Psalm 72:1-7, 10-14
January 6, 2007   Ephesians 3:1-12   **Matthew 2:1-12**

Eternal God, we thank you on this first Sunday of the year that you have never given up on us. Such as we are you are still perfecting us. We thank you that even in spite of our tardiness in growing in grace, in Jesus you have embraced us in all of our sinfulness. And you gently lead us onward. We come before you today with some very specific requests.

- Grow our hearts more generous in order that we might forgive those to whom we are so little inclined to want to extend mercy.
- Help us to release those resentments which we so consistently nurture and tightly embrace.
- Temper the watchful-eye attitude within us which sees so glaringly the offences and mistakes of our sisters and brothers.
- Without diminishing our passion for righteousness give us gentle and gracious spirits which make room for, rather than alienation from, those who wrong and sin against us.

Be also with the world of nations. We are reminded by the behaviour of Herod how tenuous is the thread by which power is held and how the threat of power lost causes people to do what normally would be unthinkable. Be in all of those places where people seek like the Maji to journey to find Jesus, child of hope. Be with all who follow the bright stars of their lives and wish freedom and peace. Be with all who live with the threats of reprisal, persecution, or danger because of their beliefs. Be with all leaders and temper their power with justice and love for people. O God, may the tragedies of the past not be repeated. May there be peace and good will among all people and may their journeys through life not be interrupted by tyrants. Amen

Eternal God of the ages, we would bow as empty vessels waiting
to be filled but our minds and souls are busy with many things which
impede our being filled by you. We become preoccupied with our
worries.

- We worry about our children.
- We worry about our personal finances.
- We worry about how well we will perform our duties.
- We worry about our health.
- We worry about terror in our world.
- We worry about war.

Help us to divest ourselves of the cares and troubles which so daily
beset us. Empty us of them now that we may be filled.

- May we be filled with a sense of your presence.
- May we be filled with the touch of your spirit.
- May we be filled with new energy.
- May we be filled with your power.
- May we be filled with trust and faith.

Empower us as we worship here and then enable us to impact
your world for Jesus. Change the stagnant water of our lives to wine
and touch us as you touched those people in Cana.

Do be with our men and women in harms way and all those
touched by the tragedy of war. Give them strength for each day as
daily they must live with terror. Give to the leaders of our world the
resolve to wage war not on people but on poverty, injustice, hunger,
disease, and all manner of human suffering. Give them the vision to
shape a new world where self-interest is tempered and corrected by
love and compassion and a hunger for justice. Give to all the world
the gift of being filled with new wine and new vision. Amen

Our gracious eternal God, the same yesterday, today and forever, we thank you that we are privileged to be alive. We so often get our religion wrong and think it expects of us sadness and loathing such as we heard about in Nehemiah's time. Help us to correct this negativity and embrace life. Teach us better how to live one day at a time and not to wish the moments away. May we not be so dissatisfied with any present moment that we violate life by wishing life away. May we not be imprisoned by the past, whether it be some bitterness we harbour, some failure or disappointment we experienced, some resentment which lingers, or some unkindness received. Help us to bury those negative things of the past and to be done with them and to go forward welcoming each new day and laying claim to the new life in Christ Jesus.

- Bring to us a sense of inner peace which comes from your power.
- Bring to us a sense of wonder and joy in the practice of our faith.
- Bring to us courage for the challenges which come our way.
- And bring to us a commitment to one another which is so strong that differences will not shake or fracture our sense of community.

Visit those whose lives are in jeopardy: those who are ill; those suffering the lingering pains of grief; those who must face life with deficits and limitations which diminish life's joys and freedoms; those whose retirement finds one spouse in the role of being a caregiver. Use us in providing ministry and comfort for them.

Bless also our world, our world leaders, and all peoples of the earth so that good will, justice, and peace may be realized. Amen

Eternal God, we bow today and ask that you would replenish our spirits.

- If we have come this day in dullness or fatigue make music in our souls.
- If we have come disconsolate lift our spirits.
- If we have come with few expectations shake us and surprise us until there are hallelujahs and praise coming from the depths of our being.
- If we have come as Jeremiah with lack of confidence and resistance bolster our spirits.

We thank you for Jeremiah's words and for the richness of the biblical heritage with its reminders of the potential we hold within us. May we not try to opt out or excuse ourselves from service because we feel inadequate as did Jeremiah. May we not try to opt out of the responsibilities of our call because of difficulty. Instead, lead us onward and cause us to grow and to reach for gains not yet realized. We thank you for the reminders that our lives are intended for rich community, fellowship, and for challenges which sometimes look too great to commence. We ask for your continued strength as we reach for a greater mastery of life.

- When we are timid give us courage.
- When we are anxious give us peace.
- When we falter gently nudge us to continue.
- When are offended enable us to forgive.
- When we are discouraged uplift our spirits and enable us to claim the victorious spirit of the faithful.

Be with those undergoing difficulty coping with life just now, especially those who might be experiencing a dark night of the soul and those who have undergone disappointment. Give them strength. Amen

Eternal God, we come to you in need of confession. For all of our sophistication in technology and progress in culture we are still woefully primitive in our spirits. Like Isaiah we cannot stifle that inner wail of "Woe is me! I am lost, for I am one of unclean lips; and I live among a people of unclean lips." We so easily fall into aimlessness and sin.

We are so uncomfortable with our own interior darkness and shadow that we project onto others and point to their sins, failings, and shortcomings. We are frightened and cannot bear to look within, so the flaws of others jump out at us.

Teach us to be less judgmental.

We find it easier to look for someone else to blame when something goes wrong and work to avoid any personal responsibility.

Teach us how to repent and to turn about.

We demonize those whose views are different than our own and in idolatrous fashion we identify you with our causes.

Teach us how to be tolerant and develop respect for others.

We so often hear messages from others out of our own personal history and limited perception and we just plain get it wrong because we put the worst spin on it.

Teach us how to interact with others, to clarify before jumping to judgment, and to find the truth.

Deliver us from the sin which would so easily beset us, gracious God. And give us the courage in confession to know that we are redeemed. Give us the power to live boldly as your redeemed people. Give to us the sense that on this day we have seen you who are high and lifted up and because of that are empowered to be your faithful people. May we go forth knowing that our guilt has been removed and our sin forgiven. Amen

O God, almighty and eternal, who crafted our universe, the suns, the earth, the moon and the stars, and all of the beautiful topography of our magnificent planet, we are in awe of your power and majesty. We find it astounding that in your greatness and majesty you have made yourself known in the gentle image of a gracious parent. We bow before you in gratitude and humble adoration and we offer you our praise and thanksgiving.

We confess that we often find ourselves living in darkness and in the shadows of life. Fearful of our own shadow we nonetheless find it comfortable to live in life's shadows. We too often forget that we are the cause of Jesus' journey. We nitpick like the Scribes who criticized Jesus for healing on the Sabbath. We too often are glad we are not as other people. We take pride in our righteousness and accomplishments, forgetting that it is you alone who make righteous. We take pride in the good things we do. We take pride in what we regard as our good motives and impugn the worst of motives to others. We hear the beatitudes but often have little enthusiasm for practicing them.

O LAMB OF GOD, WHO TAKES AWAY THE SIN OF THE WORLD, HAVE MERCY UPON US.

Save us from the foolishness of our hearts which would move toward the shadows. Give us the courage to own the sin which so easily besets us and to know once again the power of your grace to embrace us and to save and transform.

Likewise, give us grace-filled spirits and cause us to be less condemning of others, less judgmental and rejecting, less exclusive, and less inclined to build walls between ourselves and others.

We ask your care and comfort for the suffering: those whose lives are interrupted by illness, those whose family fabric has been torn by grief, those whose diminishing health is causing change or transition. Amen

Transfiguration Sunday   Exodus 34:29-35   Psalm 99
Feb. 18, 2007   2 Cor. 3:12-4:2 **Luke 9:28-36(37-43)**

O holy One, we bow before the mystery of your workings in Jesus. Like the disciples of old we too have great difficulty in moving from the old to the new. We want to frame things in ways we can understand even though the mystery is beyond words and beyond description. We are bound by our limited past and our limited conceptions. Lead us this day to the place where all things are made new. Lead us to the mountain top as Jesus led his disciples.

- Lead us to the mountain top where we can be changed.
- Lead us to the mountain top where we can have a vision of a world made new.
- Lead us to the mountain top where we can have our limited vision corrected.
- Lead us to the mountain top where we might hear the radical voice and leading of Jesus.
- Lead us to the mountain top where we can see more clearly the tasks to which you call us.
- Lead us to the mountain top where we can be commissioned to go and serve this world even as did Jesus after his descent.

LEAD US, O GOD, TO THE MOUNTAIN TOP!

Give to us the vision and the will to embrace this world of need. Where any of your people suffer we pray for a way to assist them. Where any of your people are sick we pray for the opportunity to visit them. Where any of your people hunger we pray for a way to feed them. Where any of your people are oppressed we pray for a way to provide them with justice. Where any of your people are in poverty we pray for a way to build an economic order that provides them opportunity. Be with your church throughout the world. Help us to go together to the mountain top and to join hand in hand to serve this world and to present it with the good news. Amen

First Sunday in Lent   Deuteronomy 26:1-11 Psalm 91:1-2, 9-16
Feb. 25, 2007   Romans 10:8b-13   **Luke 4:1-13**

Eternal God, as we begin our Lenten journey we come as beggars needing to be filled. We come from that metaphoric dry and thirsty land. We come from a culture which favours conflict over compassion. We come from a culture which favours toughness over tenderness. We come with all of the same temptations humankind have ever faced.

- We struggle for bread but so often fail to acknowledge that it is not by bread alone we live. We live with an anxious inner world because we are so unable to trust.
- We strive for power and influence but so often we allow a part of our inner selves to be corrupted when we gain it.
- We search for faith but so often we demand a certainty which can never be found. And we expect you to meet some test in order to give us certainty.

We live so often and so long in the wilderness of these common temptations. Forgive our foolishness. Help us to identify these temptations when they come so subtly to us. Help us to overcome them. May we not be seduced by our pursuit of security. May we not be seduced by our lust for power or influence. May we not be seduced by a false or simplistic faith which lays claims to easy answers for all of life's most difficult questions. Lead us instead to integrity. Lead us to honesty. Lead us to commitment. Help us to re-focus our lives and refashion our commitments as we journey toward the cross. Teach us to be compassionate to all of your children. Teach us to withhold our rush to judgment of others. Teach us to re-order our interior lives when they become too jumbled and noisy. Walk with us when we are fearful and frightened and when life is dark. And in such moments help us to trust that you are indeed beside us. Amen

Second Sunday in Lent Genesis 15:1-12, 17-18 Psalm 27
March 4, 2007   Philippians 3:17-4:1 **Luke 13:31-35** or
          Luke 9:28-36

Eternal God, we are so aware today that we are a part of the biblical story. We share the same dynamics as the ancients in our text today.

- We are as prone as they were to fight and destroy that which we oppose.
- We are as prone as they were to resist the truth which would enlighten us and set us free.
- We are as prone as they were to struggle against the new.
- We are as prone as they were to resist changes which would cause us to re-orient our lives and turn around and repent.

FORGIVE US OUR FOOLISH AND STUBBORN WAYS. Give us gentle rather than violent hearts. Make us teachable and open to change and growth. Deepen our understanding of life, of ourselves, and of others. Deepen our understanding of our need for a faith which goes beyond the superficial. Make us hungry for a faith which motivates us to stand with every human being and claim that person as a brother or sister. Save us from the tendency to separate people into good or evil, friend or adversary. Instead, give us a faith which causes us to have unity with all people. Make us teachable, O God, who in Jesus would have gathered all people to be taught. Prevent us from turning away as did Jerusalem.

Help us to perceive your grace throughout all of life. May we see your grace in the kindnesses of humankind. May we see your grace in the welcoming smiles of children and the elderly. May we see your grace in those who struggle with difficult diseases and who face them with courage and hope. May we see your grace wherever your people gather to sing and to share and to pray. Amen

122

Our gracious God, we sometimes come before you bored and apathetic. We sometimes have no greater expectation than getting through the day. We sometimes get lost in the business and demands and pressures of life. We become weary with the sameness of the days. Be patient with us as with the fig tree whose growth was stunted.

We ask that you surprise us today. Surprise us with the good news that our lives can be renewed. Open to us your amazing love that keeps knocking at the door of our hearts so that our praise and adoration may leap excitedly from the depths of our souls today. Open our minds to the wonder which exists in our world and our universe that we may stand in awe of your majestic creation. Open our spirits which often linger in the far country of resentment that we may behold what manner of graciousness you have manifest to us and to our human family. As we behold your graciousness cause us truly to be grateful. With eyes wide open to the darkness of life may we nonetheless aspire to life's grandeur.

Our world is heavy this week. All of Europe is fearful in the wake of the deadly bombings in Spain. We ask your healing presence among the wounded, we ask comfort for the grieving, and we ask resolve and fortitude for our nation. Be with the world of nations as it copes with those who have abandoned all human decency and intentionally slaughter the innocent. May they be brought to justice, but may we in turn be saved from a seething hatred which would consume us. Save us from the sin which would so easily beset us and make us a revengeful, hateful people. Increase our resolve to create a world in which there is greater justice for all, where no child goes to bed hungry at night, where the strong do not prey upon the weak, and where love and respect and tolerance become normative behaviours of all people. Amen

Eternal God, divine parent, whom Jesus so frequently called Father, we thank you for the qualities of that metaphor which have brought such meaning to our lives.

- We thank you that we have known you as one who knows our needs before we ask.
- We thank you that you have been for us the waiting Father who has waited like a divine parent and longed for our return from the far countries of our souls.
- We thank you that you have rejoiced at our return and welcomed us back to the family of God as you did the Prodigal Son.
- We thank you that you are still our redeeming Father and the Mother who broods over her young, and rejoice more over one repentant sinner than those already in the fold.

We ask that you would enrich all those who have the role of Father in their families. Make us all loving, understanding, accepting, and gracious among our families.

For those who have known brokenness and whose father parental model was dysfunctional bring healing and wholeness. May we never use the fact that our families were not perfect as an excuse from making a fresh start and doing better for our own families. May we seize today and resolve to make a fresh start and develop new and healthier behaviours. Give us the strength to transcend the sins of our parents that they not be repeated to the fourth and fifth generations. Bless all the families of the earth with harmony, peace, and well being and keep them from want and suffering. Help them all to love the wayward, to rejoice when one who has stumbled changes, to transcend envy and jealousy, and to promote openness and love. Amen

Our gracious, eternal God, we bow before you in awe, wonder, and with some confusion. We have heard once again the story of a woman deeply devoted to Jesus. It makes us wonder.

- We wonder how we might possibly have her kind of love and devotion.
- We wonder how we might possibly have her kind of generosity.
- We wonder how we might possibly have her kind of humility.
- We wonder how we might possibly have her kind of graciousness and hospitality to you and also to the least of your children.
- And yes, we wonder how our practical, prudential side of us could possibly give such a lavish gift just for the love of giving.

O GOD, TEACH US THE LESSONS OF MARY'S LOVING ACT.

- Teach us to see through the trappings of our religious faith to its deeper meanings.
- Teach us somehow to grow more generous and giving spirits.
- Teach us how to give hospitality and welcome to the strangers and the struggling and the broken who come into our lives.
- Teach us the gift of humility.
- Teach us to bow, to love, to worship, to adore, and then to know that this is our true purpose as your children.
- Teach us how to sacrifice and how to provide blessing for those we meet even as Mary provided blessing for Jesus.

O GOD, TEACH US THE LESSONS OF MARY'S LOVING ACT.
Amen

O eternal One, shrouded in mystery, yet revealed in Jesus; awesome in power, yet preferring to relate to us in gentleness; capable of commanding us, yet preferring to win us with love; we can but bow in awe, in wonder, in adoration, and in praise to you who are from age to age and into all of the ages.

- We thank you for that humble ride Jesus took into Jerusalem. Like those folk who greeted him that day we wish to make him fit into our preconceptions. They were wishing a conqueror. Instead he came as a gentle peacemaker.
- We would wish him to be the one who blesses our wars; instead he loves all people equally.
- We would wish him to make himself and you crystal clear and remove the ambiguity from life; instead he offers us a way and a path and the opportunity to walk by faith and the necessity to exercise simple trust.
- We would wish him to remove all sin and darkness from life; instead he offers us forgiveness.
- We would wish him to remove life's obstacles and sufferings; instead he offers us his presence in trial and rejoicing.

Be with us on this day, O God. May we be open to this life-changing Jesus. Cause us to be receptive of heart as we lean into this holy week. Teach us to temper our internal tantrums and demands and lead us to understand that most difficult virtue of humility.

Be with those who are confronting life-changing situations. Be with those with chronic and debilitating illness whose grief and loss and frustration are compounded as their physical powers wane. Be with those who have drunk the bitter cup of grief. Be to them a powerful presence. Bind up their wounds and grant them comfort. And bring our world peace, O Prince of Peace. Amen

Easter Day   Acts 10:34-43 or *Isaiah 65:17-25*   Psalm 118:1-2, 14-24
April 8, 2007   1 Cor. 15:19-26 or *Acts 10:34-43*
                  John 20 *or **Luke 24:1-12***

Our gracious, eternal God, like those women who first arrived at the empty tomb we bow on this Easter day in awe and amazement. Yet we confess that sometimes in our journey we are like the disciples to whom these women went. Upon hearing the story they thought it an idle tale and did not believe it. Like them we have difficulty, O God, in embracing new truth and new realities. When the new comes we sometimes persist in living in the old. Be with us as we vacillate between thinking the gospel an idle tale and bowing in utter amazement. Lead us to embrace this living Lord who goes before us into the streets and places of our lives even as he went before the disciples to Galilee.

Be our companion on our journey just now. The world has presented us so much bad news of late. We hear daily of our soldiers, of nationals from other countries, and of innocent bystanders dying from the world's hostilities. They are mostly numbers of people to us because we do not personally know them. Yet they are beloved by their families. Be with those left behind who reluctantly have had to learn the language and emotion of grief and loss. Grant them comfort. Bring peace where now there is hostility and chaos. Bolster us, living daily in a world of conflict, when we are tempted to succumb to moments of despair. May we lay claim to the victory of the living Jesus. May we make the conscious choice to live with hope in our hearts. May we not tire of confidently claiming that this is still your world. And may we always remember Jesus' assertion that he has overcome the world. Lead us in living confidently. Assist us in being a part of a great Christian force which brings healing to the human spirit, joy to places of sadness, and laughter to our broken world. Guide us, O Prince of Peace. Amen

Eternal God, we thank you for this Eastertide. We thank you for your victory over defeat and death, for rekindling our hope, and for rescuing us from despair and cynicism. We thank you for the indomitable spirit of those who have gone before us.

- We thank you for those who have both kept the faith alive and been kept by it.
- We thank you for those who have gone through the darkness and refused to succumb to it.
- We thank you for those who have helped resurrect our spirits by their examples and who have blessed us by believing in us when we had only hints of, but no confidence in, our own gifts.
- We thank you for Jesus who lives and reigns with you both now and forevermore.

Accompany us on our faith journey.

- Be our strength in all times of testing and trial.
- Be our guide when the road ahead seems veiled.
- Be our rock when the ground beneath us beings to shake and then whisper to us your "Peace be with you."
- Be our support when we doubt and waver.
- Be our confidence when we hear Jesus' words, "As the Father has sent me, so I send you."

O God, give us your Holy Spirit to direct us, to sustain us, and to fulfill our mission. Continue to resurrect our souls. Temper our spirits and fill us with compassion, love and understanding toward the least of your children. Give us a new vision of a world remade and refashioned on justice and equity. Give us the will to make it happen and always to remember that we are under a mandate. May we hear again Jesus' words: "...so I send you." Amen

O God, we hear the ancient challenge of Jesus to Peter reverberating through our history and challenging us once again as he asked Peter if he loved him. We too struggle and squirm for an honest answer.

- Do we love you enough to reorder our lives and set new priorities for ourselves?
  GIVE US THE COURAGE TO ANSWER HONESTLY.
- Do we love you enough to feed your lambs, to tend your sheep, to feed your sheep?
  GIVE US THE COURAGE TO ANSWER HONESTLY.
- Do we love you enough to love people and not possessions?
  GIVE US THE COURAGE TO ANSWER HONESTLY.
- Do we love you enough to commit a portion of our time and talents to serving others?
  GIVE US THE COURAGE TO ANSWER HONESTLY.
- Do we love you enough to sacrifice and to share the goods we possess in order that those who are deprived may have a place at life's table, an opportunity to gain an education, and a chance to know justice?
  GIVE US THE COURAGE TO ANSWER HONESTLY.
- Do we love you enough to proclaim to the world the hope and vision of our faith?
  GIVE US THE COURAGE TO ANSWER HONESTLY.

Gentle Jesus, may we hear your challenge to love wherever you call us to encounter our sisters and brothers. Break through our obtuseness and our resistance and persist in challenging us as you persisted with Peter. Lead us in our commitment to follow you. Lead us to say with our actions: "Yes, Lord, you know that I love you." May we invite others to share in your eternal banquet. Amen

Our gracious, eternal God, as we bow our hearts in your presence we bow in need of your graciousness. We live in a world where there is often little tolerance and compassion among human kind. We do not do well with diversity. Our history is replete with rejecting behaviours which have shut out people due to their religious beliefs, due sometimes to the color of their skin, due sometimes to their national origin, due sometimes to their sexual orientation, and due sometimes just to stubborn dislike. We bow in need of your forgiveness and grace. Forgive us our rejecting behaviours. Forgive us the rigid attitudes of our hearts which would shut out even one of your children.

We pray that you would change our hearts. Drive out the fears which so easily beset us. For fear is always what causes us to retreat from and reject others and it is fear that holds us back from embracing them.

- Give us a heart like Jesus, a receiving and gracious heart.
- Give us hearts which reach out to embrace others.
- Give us wide open arms to embrace the pain of the exile in our midst.
- Give us the will to be a church which is a gathering of the wounded, the vulnerable; yes, and also of the hopeful, those who are hopeful of a new and exciting life and a new community in Jesus the Christ.

We also bring before you the great pain and travail of our broken and war-torn world. Be with the wounded and the suffering. Be among the grieving. Be with soldiers who have served too long and yet must stay on duty because they cannot be relieved. Be with the sadistic who find delight in others' suffering. In all of that sinfulness may a new world be born. Amen

Eternal God, gracious and loving divine parent of us all, brooding over your creation with an everlasting love, we give you thanks this day for so many things:

- for the families of our origins;
- for nurturing mothers and fathers and for our children;
- for those who have nurtured us in the faith;
- for those who have faithfully offered their gifts in the various ministries of the church;
- for all who contribute to the enriching of our lives, our minds, our faith;
- for a culture which provides so many opportunities for mental and spiritual stimulation and growth.

We are of all people so richly blessed. And we give you thanks for planting us here.

We ask your blessing on our fragile world. Be with those who command others and cause them to be faithful in much. Be with those who are under orders or subordinate and may they be faithful in lesser tasks. Be with those who have lost their way and betrayed their better selves. Restore faith and renew visions and lead us to a better world.

- Give us a world where there is greater justice.
- Give us a world where the strong aid the weak.
- Give us a world where no-one and no child is hungry at night.
- Give us a world where there is safety and all of your children can lie down in peace.
- Give us a world where we share the vision and dream of Peter and dare not to presume to call unclean any of your created children.
- Give us a world where we make no distinction between people based on race or nationality and we accept everyone as your child. Amen

Eternal One, you provide hope for your people in the most difficult of times and in Jesus gave us the promise of peace.

- Be with us when our hope has worn thin.
- Be with us when we wonder about tomorrow.
- Be with us when the events of life cause us to question and wonder about your ways.
- Be with us when there is injustice among any of your people.

In such times cause us to experience your power that we might be renewed. Remind us of those comforting words of peace which you brought so gently to your friends when they were afraid of the future. May those words register with our souls and overcome our resistance.

- We resist and oftentimes shrink back from the new.
- We resist and prefer to linger in the old because even when the old is worn out and ceases to work at least it is familiar and comfortable.
- We resist the new because it might involve us in changes which we are not sure we can master and achieve.
- We resist the new because it might involve us with people with whom we are uncomfortable.

O God of the new, O God of change, O God of adventure, O God of all peoples, make all things new, you who made your home with mortals and dwelt and dwell among us.

Deepen our ability to trust. Deepen our ability to take one day at a time. Deepen our ability to love. Deepen our ability to entrust all of our dear ones to you. Deepen our sense that this is your world and that you love it and brood over it even still. Deepen our compassion for all who suffer. Amen

Most gracious God, enshrouded in awesome majesty, we have need of confession whenever we bow to recognize your presence and to listen to your beckoning.

We are so much like the disciples of old.

- We disclaim our own power and underestimate the gifts which you have so graciously bestowed upon us.
- We want to turn things over to you rather than own the challenges which you place squarely before us.
- We want some divine intervention from you to set the world right rather than working for justice, peace, and good will among all your peoples.

Forgive our foolishness. Help us to lay claim to the promise Jesus made to his friends that they too would receive power to be his witnesses. May we too receive the power to be your witnesses to our time and our world. Give us a vision worthy of our time, our talents, and our best efforts, so that we might lean toward the day when your reign is recognized by all people and all people regard others as your children, as sisters and brothers.

We thank you for those young people among us who will be having a commencement and graduation. Open to them new and exciting possibilities for the future. May their challenges be enough to force them to grow but not so great as to overwhelm them. Make their lives full. Give them courage to engage the world and to fashion it better than previous generations. Give them a vision of a world of love and of peace and the commitment to make it happen.

We also ask that you would be in all of the suffering points of your people everywhere. Be with the sick and the dying. Be with the people who must make war. Be with those who nurture hatred. Be with those suffering innocently in war zones. Grant to all your comfort and healing and peace. Amen

Day of Pentecost   **Acts 2:1-21** or *Genesis 11:1-9*   Psalm 104:24-34, 35b
May 27, 2007   Romans 8:14-17 or *Acts 2:1-21*   John 14:8-17, (25-27)

Our gracious, mysterious God, God of the wind, God of the Spirit, God of mystery, continue to invade our spirits with your powerful spirit. For in that one long ago powerful Pentecost moment, that unscrambling of the confusion of languages, all who were present were able to comprehend and understand.

However you come, whether in the wind, or whether in the silence, we need your help, O God. Bring to us and our world Pentecost moments when the myriad peoples of the earth, representing differing cultures and languages, hear one another with clarity and understanding and unity. For even using one common language we so frequently fail to understand. We confuse one another not so much with nuances of language but with nuances of deception and intention. We use words in our culture to spin stories to our ends, to hide and conceal the truth, to impose our truth on others. We refuse to listen to the truth of others and we forget your promise that the truth will set us free. Save us. Bring us Pentecost moments.

We bring before you those whose lives are punctuated with stress, dread, and terror.

- Be with those who are held hostage in the struggle in the Middle East.
- Be with their families who think the worst.
- Be with those in prison there.
- Be with those in our armed forces whose lives are constantly in danger.
- Be with our enemies who are so consumed with hatred and save us from succumbing to hatred.

To them and to us bring Pentecost moments so that one day we might all comprehend and understand completely and know the unity of the spirit. Amen

| **Trinity Sunday** | Proverbs 8:1-4, 22-31 | Psalm 8 |
| June 3, 2007 | Romans 5:1-5 | **John 16:12-15** |

O holy one, ever mysterious to us, yet ever in and among us, we thank you for your placing within us a quest for truth. We thank you for your hidden prodding toward new discoveries. We thank you that however much we gain of the truth we still remain unfinished because life is always an up and down journey and we cannot contain it all. Be with us on our journey and lead us as the disciples were led to embrace new and exciting truths as we are able to receive them.

- Lead us in those times of stagnation when we feel nothing is happening and when we seem to be stuck in place.
- Lead us in those times when discouragement seems to overwhelm us and we think the quest for truth is futile.
- Lead us in those times when a new idea threatens some of our long-held beliefs and we become fearful.
- Lead us in those times when the light dawns on some new idea or truth and we become excited and renewed.
- Lead in those times when a truth we hold dear comes in conflict with a truth someone else holds dear and there is conflict. In such times help us to be gracious and open rather than judgmental and rejecting.
- Lead us ever onward with the confidence that you have "more light and truth to reveal to us from your word." (John Robinson)

May your spirit lead us onward, be patient with us, and lead us into all truth. Be with the church and all faiths throughout the earth and help us to engage in respectful dialogue and come to greater understanding and unity of spirit. Amen

1 Kings 17:8-16, (17-24) or *I Kings 17:17-24*

Psalm 46 or *Psalm 30*   Galatians 1:11-24

Luke 7:11-17

Our gracious, eternal God, we bow today having heard an event which creates for us a great mystery. Our minds cannot get around what happened that day in Nain when Jesus returned an only son to his mother. We can only bow and wonder about this Jesus.

- We wonder about what kind of power he had.
- We wonder about why he chose this particular woman among all others who needed his attention.
- We wonder about the depth of his compassion for our sorrows and how you must love us with a healing love.
- We wonder about those carrying the boy who were stopped in their tracks when Jesus came forward.

Our questioning minds can only wonder. They cannot get around such a powerful happening. We can, however, thank you for the compassion you have for all who bear grief. We can identify with this sorrowing woman. We can also identify with the boy for we are in need figuratively of arising from all that is dead in our lives.

- We are in need of arising from the slumber of lethargy about our faith.
- We are in need of arising from the slumber of insensitivity to human need throughout the earth.
- We are in need of arising from the slumber of prejudice, discrimination and racism which has so long infected our land.
- We are in need of arising from the slumber of failing to work for peace.
- We are in need of arising from the slumber of sloth and neglect of the great commission.

O God, help us to arise. Touch us that we may arise to life.
Amen

Proper 6 (11)   1 Kings 21:1-10, (11-14), 15-21a or *2 Sam. 11:26 12:10, 13-15*
June 17, 2007   Psalm 5:1-8 or *Psalm 32*   **Galatians 2:15-21**
                      Luke 7:36-8:3

O holy one, we bow today so aware of our tendencies and efforts to diminish the gospel of Jesus. We get occasional glimpses of your grace but we so often fail to grasp its wideness and we fall back into a religion of law.

- Jesus proclaimed the possibility of a radical faith and trust while we try to make faith more certain and controllable.
- Jesus proclaimed freedom of the spirit while we find it easier to live by surface rules which serve as a flight from anxiety and ambiguity.
- Jesus summed up all law in the word love but we put limits on whom we will love and we cast a long shadow of judgment over many people we meet.

O God, from the time of the Galatians your church has often been losing its way. Your grace is so abundant; yet we retreat into the world of law. We build systems and rules which are intended to rule out people who do not live as we think they ought. Grant us your healing touch. Remind us, O God, that we are justified and made yours only through your grace and graciousness.

- Help us to remember that we cannot buy or bargain or bully our way to righteousness by our own efforts.
- Help us to remember that it is only through faith that we are made whole.
- Help us to remember that your grace is granted to all people and that we are called to have generous and receiving spirits as we encounter others of your children on our journeys.
- Help us to put aside the old calculating self and walk with freedom and faith and renewed joy. Amen

137

THIS PRAYER IS BASED ON THE GOSPEL FOR JUNE 17

Eternal God, we are reminded today of so many of our internal issues which continue to plague us and just won't go away. We are reminded of some of the worst sides of humanity, yet still they persist among all of us.

- We are so like Simon, liking propriety and looking down on the outcast.
- We are so judgmental that when confronted with a flagrant sinner we recoil into a satisfied kind of self-righteousness.
- We are inclined to hold onto the superficial trappings of our faith and to miss the reality and depth of your forgiving grace.
- We are so fearful of the potential evil that lurks in our own souls that we find it easy to behold it in others where it is so much more glaring.
- We are inclined both to miss the reality of grace and to deny it to others.

O GOD, FORGIVE US OUR BEGRUDGING AND REJECTING SPIRITS. We do not wish to remain this way. We wish to grow larger, more accepting spirits.

- Help us come to a deeper understanding of your profound and loving graciousness and grace which you offer the worst of sinners.
- Help us to take the edge off our so prevalent rejecting reactions.
- Help us to develop behaviours which are welcoming and accepting to each person you place in our path.
- Help us to love all of your children and not do violence to the undeserving because we are all undeserving. Amen

Proper 7 (12)   1 Kings 19:1-4, (5-7), 8-15a or *Isaiah 65:1-9*
June 24, 2007   Psalm 42 and 43 or *Psalm 22:19-28*   **Galatians 3:23-29**
                   Luke 8:26-39

Our gracious, eternal God, we thank you for the blessings which are abundantly ours. We thank you for the gentle arrival of summer days, for azure skies and the new and varied colors in new green leaves, for gentle warm days, for all of nature which reminds us of your gracious provision for our needs, and for such a beautiful world which points us to a majestic creator God.

We thank you for the Scriptures which provide us a window into our souls and provide for spiritual growth and understanding. We are reminded today of some of the tensions with which we permanently live.

- We would live free in your grace, yet we easily succumb to wanting clear rules of law.
- We would live free in your grace, yet we often want to be justified by what we do and by our achievements and good works.
- We would live free in your grace, yet we are inclined to long for some clear statement or code which, when upheld by us, would give us the confidence and certainty that we have done all that you require of us.
- We would live free in your grace, yet we so easily divide people up into the righteous and the unrighteous, the favoured and the rejected, that we miss the gospel's truth that there are no superior Christians, but we are all united in you who love all with an everlasting love.

O God, permeate our hearts with your grace and help us to find greater room in them for others.

Breathe your gentle, healing spirit upon all this day who need your special graces and keep this world in your loving embrace. Amen

Proper 8 (13)   2 Kings 2:1-2, 6-14 or *1 Kings 19:15-16, 19-21*
July 1, 2007   Psalm 77:1-2, 11-20 or *Psalm 16*   **Galatians 5:1, 13-25**
                     Luke 9:51-62

Our gracious God, we thank you today for the land in which we live. We thank you for the freedoms which are ours, for the multitude of opportunities presented to each of us, for a land of abundance. Forgive us for our lack of creativity in sharing the nation's bounties inequitably, for tarnishing our political process with greed, for failing the needy. Save us from that litany of destructive behaviours which St. Paul outlined: enmities, strife, jealousy, anger, quarrels, dissension, factions, envy, and all that would undo us. Lead us instead to strive for the fruits of the spirit.

- Help us to develop loving behaviours which demonstrate care and compassion for others.
- Help us in an over-serious and gloomy world to know real joy because you help us overcome the world.
- Help us to work for peace in a world which seems to prefer violence.
- Help us, in our hurry up world, to develop patience and to learn that all does not have to be completed in our hurry up time.
- Help us to demonstrate kindness to all and especially to those with whom we find it especially difficult to be kind.
- Help us to learn generosity with our resources but help us especially to learn how to be generous in our attitudes and behaviours toward people.
- And help us to be faithful, gentle, and self-controlled.

O God, raise our national vision. Give us tolerance and understanding for all peoples. May we hold dear for all people the freedoms we cherish. Amen

Proper 9 (14)   2 Kings 5:1-14 or *Isaiah 66:10-14*
July 8, 2007   Psalm 30 or *Psalm 66:1-9*   Galatians 6:(1-6), 7-16
<u>**Luke 10:1-11, 16-20**</u>

Eternal God, we thank you for sunny and gentle summer days, for a world so beautiful, for long days with early sunrises and lingering evenings and spectacular sunsets. We thank you for the mountains which have varied and different looks and which are a constant reminder of whence comes our help. On such a day as this, lazy as it may seem, we ask that you would challenge us to a greater vision for which we have previously lacked courage. Remind us that in looking back we also look forward to today's challenges.

- Remind us that Jesus, supremely gifted, nonetheless called seventy others to go before him and prepare his way because he could not carry on his tasks without help.
- Remind us that we too are your hands and voice today and we are needed as were they.
- Remind us that our task as a church is not to be happily cloistered looking inward but to be your labourers in your harvest today.
- Remind us, whenever we feel inadequate for the task before us, that we are told to trust you and to step forward with boldness and trust.
- Remind us that we are called to be peacemakers and to bring the message of peace to others.
- Remind us that we have a ministry to the sick and the needy and we are called to bear your message of a victorious life to all peoples.

O God, give us power in our time. Startle us as those seventy were startled by the results of their witness. Give us power to live the good news, to proclaim the good news, and to lead and love others to the good news. Make us bold in your service. Amen

Eternal God, we come this day to hear again your Word of grace.
- We come to have you illumine the darker corners of our lives.
- We come to find comfort where we have aching, hurt, and pain.
- We come to receive once again support and love from our sisters and brothers.
- We come to receive forgiveness for our sins and failures.
- We come to be renewed for our journey.

We pray that we may know a profound sense of your love and acceptance and have confidence that we are among those who by faith know your grace.

Like the rich ruler we know the two simple commandments which sum up the law. But like him we are stung in our spirits by Jesus' story of the Good Samaritan.
- We are as prone to be repelled by people who are different as were those two who walked by and would not get involved because he was a Samaritan.
- We are as prone to be too busy to stop.
- We are as prone not to want to be bothered.
- We are as prone to want someone else to help and to wish his problem away.
- We are as prone to be insensitive to the sufferings of others.

Make us reflective in those moments when we would reject another person. Help us to choose on the side of inclusiveness and learn to curb the common human bent toward rejection and exclusiveness. Temper our hatreds. Temper our penchant for believing the worst of people. Temper our prejudices. Lead us one day to unity and peace and to love all your people. Amen

O holy one, ever trying to influence and touch the hearts of your people, we thank you today for the opportunity to pause, to worship, and to reflect upon the direction our lives are taking. We confess that we so easily lose our focus. There is so much of Martha residing within us.

- Like Martha we too often live in that land of resentment where we feel put upon and used, never quite acknowledging that it is we who choose that position.
- Like Martha we become anxious and distracted when we feel overwhelmed and we unexpectedly lash out at those around us.
- Like Martha we become distracted from where our true focus ought to be and we get lost in a whirlwind of details.
- Like Martha we often fail to know how to stop the downward spirals in which we find ourselves.
- Like Martha we become people of worry rather than people of trust and confidence.

Correct us and make us more like Mary.

- Make us people who are able to sort out life and set meaningful priorities.
- Make us people who are teachable and who learn from the ancient wisdom of the Word.
- Make us people who are attentive to our inner lives and who are constantly growing.
- Make us people who invest our time in others and in things which make a difference in the lives of others.

Make us people who are more like Mary. Amen

Proper 12 (17)   Hosea 1:2-10 or *Genesis 18:20-32*   Psalm 85 or *Psalm 138*
July 29, 2007   Colossians 2:6-15 (16-19)   **Luke 11:1-13**

O eternal one, we thank you for the rains which been so steady this week, reminding us that you replenish our earth. We thank you for your faithfulness to us.

We confess that we frequently do not know how to address you. Our words fail us because we fail to bring to you our complete selves. We want to present the Sunday side of ourselves and hide the chaos, frustration, and inner turmoil which are also parts of us. When we feel as bereft as did Job we fail to rage and so we fail to make contact with you. O God of the storm as well as of the peaceful quiet, teach us how to progress on our spiritual journeys.

- Teach us to pray as Jesus taught his friends.
- Teach us what is important and enable us to bring what is important to you in prayerful conversation.
- Teach us the kind of trust that confidently relies upon you to provide us our daily bread.
- Teach us about the link between asking for forgiveness and being willing to forgive others.
- Teach us how to be strong in the face of temptation.
- Teach us how to commit all to your rule, to trust your power, to behold your glory.

We pray for our nation which is engaged in political dialogue. We pray that respect and decency will prevail over what is often a rancorous process. We pray that the ancient vision of justice may be more completely realized in this land and in the world.

We also pray for our world. Where hatred prevails we pray that human hearts might change. May all peoples give up ways of relating which are destructive. We have all nurtured enmity over and over again which only pushes peace farther and farther away. Help us to give up such foolishness and work for peace. Amen

Our gracious, eternal God, we bow to you who are from everlasting to everlasting. We thank you for that seed of uneasiness which you have placed within us which causes us to hunger and thirst for an inner peace which endures. Yet we often wander on life's journey and fail to find peace. And we know that our lack of peace is due to the many ways in which we misdirect our inner discontent.

- We set our sights on money and would figuratively build bigger and better barns.
- We keep our eye upon those who are more successful and we become consumed by envy.
- We carry resentment that someone else has more than we and we rail against life's unfairness.
- We long for a security which money might bring but fail to see that there is no way money can cure our inner discontent.

Bend your ear to us this day. Provide your healing touch and help us to redirect our search for security and peace.

- Help us always to remember that it is you who lend us life and that life is a gift.
- Help us to remember that the purpose of life is always greater than knowing that we have enough for tomorrow.
- Help us to remember that our resources also are only a gift and that we are only caretakers with a responsibility for the well being of our sisters and brothers.
- Help us to remember that true riches do not lie in abundance but in being rich toward you who alone offer a peace which passes all understanding.

O God, we ask that you would transform us and provide us victory over all greed and avarice. Amen

Isaiah 1:1, 10-20 – or *Genesis 15:1-6*

Psalm 50:1-8, 22-23 or *Psalm 33:12-22*

Hebrews 11:1-3, 8-16   Luke 12:32-40

O holy One, we thank you that we stand in a long line of believers who have been faithful through the ages. You have been leading your people through trial and difficulty and have always set before them hope for today and hope for a better tomorrow. We pray that you would bless us in our time as we seek to be as faithful as our forebears. May we too know the faith which is filled with hope in things not seen.

- Give to us a faith like the grain of mustard seed which had small beginnings but which yielded large results.
- Give to us the faith to move the mountains of difficulty which come to each of us.
- Give to us the faith that sees a distant goal and is willing to work to achieve it.
- Give to us a faith which has a vision of a new world where peace and love characterize the transactions of people and of nations and where war is no more.
- Give to us a faith such as Abraham's to move forward not knowing our destination but trusting in your guiding providence.
- Give to us a faith which is able to endure those moments of personal disquiet and to trust that you are with us.
- Give to us a faith which sees the welfare of humankind as our business because it is the focus of your enduring love for your people.
- Give to us a faith which sees beyond the years to an eternal city.

O God, give us faith to walk with you through the ebb and flow and the victories and the defeats of life and to achieve victory and mastery of life. Amen

Proper 15 (20)	Isaiah 5:1-7 or *Jeremiah 23:23-29*
August 19, 2007	Psalm 80:1,2,8-19 or *Psalm 82*
	Hebrews 11:19-12:2 Luke 12:49-56

Our gracious, eternal God, we pause with gratitude on this late August Sunday. We thank you for the land in which we live and which is now yielding bountiful harvests. We thank you for the abundance of foods and the many choices available to us. We have been abundantly blessed in this nation of ours and we thank you.

As we reflect on life we know that most of us will be little remembered in future generations. We will not be mentioned in an enduring book as were Rahab, Gideon, Barak, Samson, David, and that host of others who were given as examples of people of outstanding faith. Yet we pray that you would nonetheless make us people of outstanding faith.

- Give us the vision to work for a world where all people share the abundance we have known and where none of your children is without.
- Give us the vision to fashion a world where discrimination is no longer rampant.
- Give us the vision of a world where there is acceptance and love and affirmation expressed to the least of your children.
- Give us the vision to create a world where there is respect granted by people of all faiths for all others.
- Give us the vision to work for a world of justice and peace.

O God, surrounded as we are by that great cloud of witnesses which has gone before us, grant us courage to forge forward in faith and hope in our time. Help us to set aside all pride, all concern to be remembered or recognized, and help us to be faithful to the heavenly calling. Help us to run the race set before us. Amen

O God of graciousness, we bow ever astonished by your lavish bestowal of love, grace, and tenderness to us. Indelibly etched in the good news of Jesus is your loving acceptance of the wayward, the rebellious, the broken, and the contrite. Cause us likewise to extend that loving acceptance to those whom we meet on our daily journey. Save us from the self-righteous, condemning attitude exhibited by the leader of the synagogue that day when Jesus healed on the Sabbath day. We confess that it is an attitude which we oftentimes exhibit. Save us from the false security that somehow our truth is the only truth, that our understandings are the only right ones, and that we hold control over your mysterious workings in humankind. Save us from building barriers when we should be building bridges and partnerships. Be with us on our life journeys.

- When our way has suddenly become hard and seemingly difficult give us grace to move forward.
- When our way has become lonely and uncertain give us grace to step forward.
- When our way holds more darkness than light give us grace to move forward.
- When we quiver inwardly give us greater courage.
- When we hurry but seemingly get nowhere give us greater patience.
- When we are overwhelmed by commitments give us trust that you will provide strength.
- When we are weary and wonder about our results give us faithfulness.

Bless our Christian community and may we all be held up by your strong and everlasting arms. Amen

Eternal God, we thank you for the opportunity of quiet reflection upon our lives and the patterns which have gained dominance in them. We thank you for the opportunity to reflect upon the focus of our lives and to hear the corrective wisdom from our faith. Give us courage to have ears to hear because our confessions are a litany of the struggles we live with daily.

- We are so much like the people of long ago, wanting to have prestige and power.
- We are so much like the people of long ago, elbowing our way to the top and the highest places of honour.
- We are so much like the people of long ago, wanting to be recognized as a cut above others.
- We are so much like the people of long ago, wanting to engage in the game of competition and beat out others.
- We are so much like the people of long ago, wanting to toot our own horns and call attention to our importance.

FORGIVE US OUR PRIDEFUL AND SINFUL WAYS. Give us a new perspective on what is important in life. Help us to see our neighbours as people to be loved and affirmed and not as people with whom we are in competition and who must be beaten. Teach us ways of humility and give us self-perspective. Help us to build self worth which is based on positive achievements rather than on power. Help us not to divide up people into those who are worthy to associate with and those who are not. May we not discriminate against any of your children. Help us, O God, to be among those who know how to humble themselves rather than to be among those who constantly seek to call attention to themselves. Be with us in this inner struggle and help us at least to take baby steps toward humility. Amen

Proper 18 (23)
Sept. 9, 2007

Jeremiah 18:1-11 or *Deuteronomy 30:15-20*
Psalm 139:1-6, 13-18 or *Psalm 1*
Philemon 1-21   **Luke 14:25-33**

Eternal God, we bow with ambivalence during this another week of a September eleventh. The remembrance of that destructive catastrophe is indelibly seared into our souls. We confess our tendency to harbour hatred which we know is wrong. We often have felt outrage and intense anger. Aircraft have taken on a new and alien and unwanted meaning. And we have formed a very suspicious world which seems always to be on the edge of terror. Deliver us, O God, from this body of death.

Provide healing to our hatred bent world.

- Give healing to the age-old tendency to place blame for problems on someone else.
- Give healing to the age-old tendency to seek revenge, to save face, to get even.
- Give healing to the age-old and foolish notion that force and war and arms are the solution to any problem.
- Give healing to the age-old tendency of nations to desire to dominate others.

Give us greater trust in one another. Give us the will to choose love rather than hate. Give us the ability to risk on behalf of peace.

We pray for our national leaders and all of the political leaders of the world. Teach them and us new ways of relating. Heal the inevitable conflicts of the world. Teach us all where to focus the values of our hearts. Help us to be about the business of building that shining realm of God of which Jesus spoke, of counting the cost, of divesting our lives of the greed of possessions. Help us to put aside the values of the past. Help us learn to deny ourselves in the pursuit of the gospel. Help us to count the cost of our spiritual journey, to find victory, and to trust you when the way is not clear. Amen

Luke 15:1-10

Our gracious, eternal God, we thank you for this Sunday which begins a new program year for our church. Fill us today with excitement.

- Fill us with excitement for our children and young people as they begin their study and fellowship.
- Fill us with excitement for the inquiring minds of adults as we too return to more disciplined study.
- Fill us with excitement for the opportunity of stretching our minds.

We would ask your blessing on all these ventures. Deepen our faith, increase our understanding, enlarge our dreams, and further our commitment to be your faithful people in this place.

We bring before you our cares and our needs. The world continues to know episodes of violence. The level of anxiety and apprehension for many people is great. Right now the world needs your quieting and steadying peace. Bring calm to our souls when the waves of life roll high. Give us the assurance that you will meet us in every storm of life. Give us the assurance that we are always in your care. And help us to cast all of our cares upon you who love us with an everlasting love.

Continue to teach us of the depths of your love for humankind. When we are weary of evil and people we regard as evil remind us that Jesus reached out to sinners. When we feel self-content remind us that you reach out to the one who is lost and rejoice when one of your children again is found or finds the way home. Overwhelm us once again with your searching love that would not only find the lost one but would bring healing and love and forgiveness. Give to your church the love which searches for the lost. Amen

Jeremiah 8:18-9:1 or *Amos 8:4-7*
Psalm 79:1-9 or *Psalm 113*
1 Timothy 2:1-7   **Luke 16:1-13**

O holy One, we bow this day, each coming from a different place. Some bow triumphantly and feel strongly about the mastery of life. Some bow with unsettling circumstances in their lives and are uncertain, cautious. Some bow with disappointments from life. We all bow with ambivalence about the world of wealth and money and means and what it means to be a steward.

- On the one hand we want to trust you; on the other hand we struggle and strive and feel better when we are financially secure.
- On the one hand we want to use money and cherish people; on the other hand we are tempted to use others for gain.
- On the one hand we want to be able to risk for you; on the other hand we are held back by our fears about tomorrow.

Deliver us, gracious God, from this ongoing battle of trying to serve two masters. Enable us to put order and perspective into our lives, to be faithful with what you have put into our hands as a trust, and most of all to discover what true riches are. Give us joy in our gifts, wisdom in our money management, fulfillment with goals reached, and the satisfaction of joining the faithful in building your shining city.

For our war-torn and war-weary world we again ask almost the impossible. Change the hearts of warriors and of nations that we may know peace. Be with innocent civilians and children who suffer. Give us the will to put an end to war and the suffering which continues in so many places. Amen

Our gracious, eternal God, we bow today with humility and a little bit of fear. We thank you that you do not wish us to cower before you in fear, however, but to remind us that our actions and decisions carry with them a sense of accountability and they bear lasting effects. The world has many rich men but it has many more people like Lazarus. The age old saga of neglect and poverty go on and on from century to century. Help us to learn the lesson Jesus taught so long ago.

- Help us to realize that we cannot live life indifferently from those who suffer.
- Help us to realize that each of us is bound to all others.
- Help us to realize that to whom much is given much is also required.
- Help us to realize that the resources we have been given are not for our exclusive use and enjoyment but are meant to be utilized in your service and for the needy.
- Help us to realize that we are called to step forth and place our resources and our influence upon the side of justice for all people.
- Help us to realize, O God, that we are accountable to you for our life's performance.

Transform our attitudes toward money with which we all struggle. Transform us from a stingy and calculating posture to one of generosity. Transform us from insensitivity and a sense of powerlessness about poverty to people who care. Impress upon us that we who have so much can bring relief to those who hunger and suffer. Impress upon us that we are our sisters' and our brothers' keeper. Amen

Proper 22 (27)   Lamentations 1:1-6 or *Habakkuk 1:1-4, 2:1-4*
Oct. 7, 2007   Lamentations 3:19-26 or *Psalm 37.1-9*
                      2 Timothy 1:1-14   **Luke 17:5-10**

Eternal God, we are blessed to be invited to the table of our Lord with all of our Christian sisters and brothers on this world-wide communion day. May we feel the strength of your church universal. May we deepen our commitments. May we have our vision elevated. And may our mission in this time and this place be made clear.

Save your church from all sinfulness and foolishness. Help us to refrain from baptizing our opinions and prejudices and assume they are supported by the gospel. Remind us of the biblical truth that judgment begins with the house of God. Cleanse us, challenge us, lead us, so that we may be faithful to the heavenly vision.

We pray for our fragile world. Where choices are being made in hatred, where violence is being planned or perpetrated, where any human being turns away from a neighbor in anger, swing low and transform those hearts with love. Help us as your children to foreswear our penchant for war and work for peace.

We pray that you would give your church a faith which is as powerful and influential as a grain of mustard seed and whose influence is felt throughout the world.

- Give us the faith that we hold the key to a power we have left untapped.
- Give us the faith that though we individually feel we have little to offer you can multiply the effects of our efforts.
- Give us the faith that boldly puts forth our gifts and refuses to minimize them.
- Give us the faith to believe that we can overcome the world.

O God, give us faith. Amen

154

Proper 23 (28)   Jeremiah 29:1, 4-7 or *2 Kings 5:1-3, 7-15c*
Oct. 14, 2007   Psalm 66:1-12 or *Psalm 111*
                  2 Timothy 2:8-15   **Luke 17:11-19**

Our gracious, eternal God, we come this day with many needs. Some are in need of healing as were these ten who called out to Jesus and who got his attention because they called out for mercy. Some have gone through that dark valley with Job and have within them a deep protest about how life has gone for them. Laments of your unfaithfulness and abandonment sometimes lie just beneath the surface. If we are in that number we pray that you would lead us to a new depth of trust and assurance which has thus far eluded us.

Some are in need of reconciliation and a fresh start and are looking to find again the magic of love and to find a way to elevate their lives above what seems like the din of incessant conflict. If we are in that number lead us we pray to new relational behaviours. But lead us also to have changed and renewed spirits. Teach us the joy of listening to the other for understanding rather than retort. Teach us the honesty of self-disclosure rather than deception and avoidance. Teach us to find unity and oneness once again.

Some are in need of learning how to be grateful and less self-centered and are in need of learning how to say "thank you" for your great gifts. If we are in that number, like the nine men who were healed and failed to say "thank you," we struggle with taking life and its gifts and your graces for granted and assume that what we receive is our due. Yes, and sometimes life is too daily and we expect too much from life. Cause us to count our blessings and lend to all of us a heart filled with thankfulness and gratitude. Give to us a profound sense of gratitude for all of your blessings that we might say: "hallelujah." Give us the ability to look on life and to say that it is good even as you pronounced it so in creation. Give us the attitude of gratitude. Amen

Jeremiah 31:27-34 or *Genesis 32:22-31*
Psalm 119·97-104 or *Psalm 121*
2 Timothy 3:14-4:5   **Luke 18:1-8**

Our gracious, eternal God, we bow this day and again ask you to teach us to pray.

- In such times as we fail to feel your presence teach us the discipline of prayer. Rid us of any superficial demand for a feel-good faith so that our prayers are not dependent upon emotion.
- In such times as something in our lives seems hopeless teach us to pray and not to give up.
- In such times as it seems as if our words go forth but lack energy and life teach us to persist and pray even though we feel little passion.
- In such times when we despair of ever finding an answer to a vexing problem teach us to pray and give us courage to continue onward.
- In such times when we despair of prayer itself and wonder if it does any good teach us to be persistent as was that widow in Jesus' long ago story.

O God, teach us the simplicity of prayer which Jesus taught. Give us the persistence to knock on your door and to bang at your gates and not to lose heart. And when we cannot find the words to articulate our needs or those of our neighbour may your spirit intercede with utterances from the depths of our being.

We ask your gentle care for the least of your children throughout the world: for those who suffer innocently because of cruelty; for people caught in the crossfire of war and conflict; for the hungry and the homeless everywhere. Be with them and give them courage in their unwanted crisis. Give us the resolve to build a just world. Amen

Proper 25 (30)   Joel 2:23-32 or *Sirach 35:12-17* or *Jer. 14:7-10, 19-22*
Oct. 28, 2007   Psalm 65 or *Psalm 84:1-7*   2 Timothy 4:6-8, 16-18
Luke 18:9-14

Eternal God, the holy one, we are often presumptuous when we come before you. We are so often like the Pharisee who went up to pray. We feel him inside us.

- We feel him inside us when we feel that somehow we are of all your people most deserving.
- We feel him inside us when we feel that we are not needy like other people because we are so self-reliant.
- We feel him inside us when we feel that we are a cut above those with whom we live daily.
- We feel him inside us when we are uncomfortable with the evil within us and we do such a marvellous job of self deception by denying it.
- We feel him inside us when we feel that it is better to project evil onto others where we are able to see it so blatantly.

In all these ways we are the one in that story Jesus told, and in all these ways we are overcome by a pride which is unbecoming of your people. Forgive us and save us from this useless and destructive pattern. Give us the courage to pray that you would also be merciful to us because we are sinners. Grant us to find true humility of heart and spirit and the courage to look inwardly even when we fear what we may find. Help us again to discover and to believe in your grace which awaits a humble and contrite spirit. And help us to gain a faith which includes those who struggle, those who sin, those who have a ways to go. Make us into gracious people who know we live by grace and who make allowances for, rather than criticize, others. Give us generous hearts. Help us to own the humanity which we share with others and to embrace all your children. Amen

Proper 26 (31)   Habakkuk 1:1-4; 2:1-4 or *Isaiah 1:10-18*
Nov. 4, 2007   Psalm 119:137-144 or Psalm 32:1-7
                         2 Thess. 1:1-4, 11-12   **Luke 19:1-10**

Our gracious, eternal God, we thank you for the scriptures which bring us stark reminders that illumine our human situation. Today we are reminded of one Zaccheus and his powerful need to be received, to be loved, to be accepted, to be blessed, and to be forgiven. He reflects one of the deepest needs of humankind and our longings are the same as his were that day when he longed to see Jesus.

We are also reminded that we are like the crowd that day and the host of judgmental, rejecting, self-righteous people who could not bear to behold such grace and acceptance. All they could do was complain and grumble about the company Jesus was keeping that day. We confess that we are not unlike them.

- How often we feel that the wayward ought to get what they deserve.
- How often we feel people need to watch the company they keep.
- How often we feel the religious folk ought always to act religious.
- How often we feel the sinner has no right to be a part of us.
- How often with our condemning, self-righteous attitudes we place limits upon your love and grace.

In such times help us to climb above the prejudices we hold. In such times remind us that we are all children of Abraham. In such times help us to see the transforming Jesus who receives, loves, accepts, blesses, and forgives the worst of sinners and makes room for all of us in his company. Help us to see that he would come to dwell with each of us. Help us to make room for him and also for all of your children. Amen

Proper 27 (32)   Haggai 1:15b-2:9 or *Job 19:23-27a*
Nov. 11, 2007   Psalm 145:1-5, 17-21 or *Psalm 98 or Psalm 17:1-9*
                 2 Thess. 2:1-5, 13-17   **Luke 20:27-38**

Our gracious, eternal God, we come to you on this consecration Sunday needing your blessing. You ask the gift of ourselves, yet we so often think only of money. We are often ambivalent about our resources. We think of obligation rather than of opportunity. We think of duty rather than the privilege of giving of ourselves and our money. We think others, more richly blessed than we, ought to bear the greatest burden of our church's commitments. We take the joy out of sharing and we destroy the joy of feeling that we are a significant part of your work here in this church and throughout the world. Forgive us our lack of vision. Touch our hearts and teach us to give of our talents, our time, and our treasure so that we can know true joy, true peace, and true fulfillment.

We also ask your help for those times in our lives when difficulty comes. Give us the courage to meet misfortune with resolute hearts. Give us patience when answers or resolution do not come quickly. Through the anvil of life make us strong and help us to be victorious.

We offer our prayers for those who are presently going through suffering and who need your healing touch, for those whose lives know too much darkness, for those who grieve.

Be also with our troubled, violence prone world. Somehow may all of your children come to know that war is not the answer to the issues of nations or peoples. Bless our veterans who have had to endure war and bloodshed. Bless also those who currently serve in harms way in our present conflicts and bring us peace to this earth. And bless all who suffer from the consequences of war. Give them all comfort and strength. Amen

Proper 28 (33)   Isaiah 65:17-25 or *Malachi 4:1-2a*
Nov. 18, 2007   Isaiah 12 or *Psalm 98*   2 Thess. 3:6-13
                     Luke 21:5-19

THANKSGIVING SUNDAY

Our gracious eternal God, ever with us through the seasons of
the year as well as the seasons of life, we pause with thanksgiving
in our hearts this day.

- We thank you for this land, filled with resources and
  beauty, wealthy and manifestly blessed when compared
  to the nations of the earth.
- We thank you that for most of us the occasion of our birth
  placed us in this country with such great opportunity and
  not in another land where doors would be shut.
- We thank you for the way in which you have so richly
  peopled our lives and placed us in rich communities such
  as this church where we are received and accepted so
  graciously.
- We thank you for a free society with great resources and
  the opportunity to read great books, hear great music,
  exercise civic responsibility, and find fulfillment without
  government interference.

We pray for our nation as we approach our day of national
thanksgiving. Make us mindful of our past and inspire within us
the vision to perfect a still more perfect union. May our leaders be
people of vision who by their offices are led to become statesman
rather than opportunistic politicians. Give us all the vision of a world
where justice and peace and love reign and where all of your people
have their needs met. Give us thankful hearts. Amen

160

O eternal God, the alpha and the omega, the beginning and the end, we pause with sombre hearts on this last Sunday of the church year. We are especially mindful of those among us who have died and have been gathered unto you but whose departure has left gaping holes in the fabric of their families' lives. And we are mindful of those who died in war. O Christ the ruler be present to all who have suffered losses. Provide your healing comfort for the grieving and compassion through us for all who suffer.

- Provide forgiveness for the foolish ways of humankind as you provided forgiveness to those around the cross.
- Provide correction from cynicism and sarcasm and the hope for an easy remedy to things wrong such was exhibited by one of the thieves on the cross.
- Provide hope such as you provided to the other thief on the cross when you promised he would be with you in paradise.
- Provide assurance that the Jesus of the Cross will lead all of us to victory and eternal life.

O GOD, LEAD US IN THE COMING CHURCH YEAR.

- Deepen our love and commitment to you and the cause of serving humankind.
- Deepen our ability to trust and to believe in the fundamental goodness of life.
- Deepen our ability to greet each new day and see it as a gift from you and an opportunity for triumph.
- Deepen our ability to affirm our sisters and brothers in the faith and to help them to believe in themselves.
- Deepen our ability to discover and to serve the Christ in our neighbour.

O GOD, LEAD US AND BE OUR GUIDE. Amen

Made in the USA
Columbia, SC
22 February 2020

88285349R00107